FERGIE

Memoirs of a Musical Legend

FERGIE

Memoirs of a Musical Legend

Fergie MacDonald
with
Allan Henderson

First published in 2003 by
Birlinn Limited
West Newington House
10 Newington Road
Edinburgh EH9 1QS

www.birlinn.co.uk

ISBN 1 84158 284 0

British Library Cataloguing in Publication Data
A catalogue record for this book is available from the British Library

Typeset in Berthold Garamond by Brinnoven, Livingston
Printed and bound by Creative Print and Design, Wales

Which Fergie?

All the horses were gone from the croft and the hill
They'd invented a tractor to furrow the drill
It was sturdy and neat, some are going strong still
The Grey Fergie

When Randy Prince Andy decided to wed
He'd the pick of the rich and the very well-bred
H.M. and the Duke weren't amused when instead
He took flaming-haired Sarah
His Fergie

From sport's humble beginnings to the 'Land's Richest' list
He's pushed many to goals they'd have otherwise missed
On touchline and pitch he's been cheered, he's been hissed
He's Sir Fergie

But one far above these and we all will agree
Be it *Talla a Bhaile*, radio or TV
With that smile on his face and the box on his knee
He's our Fergie

Catriona Tawse

Contents

List of Illustrations

Foreword

It only takes the simple mention of the name Fergie MacDonald to elicit a warm and friendly response from the audience. For the last ten years or so, the music and stories of Fergie have played a pivotal role in our concerts. His music is filled with the same spirit as the man himself.

Many of the tunes I have learned from him were delivered by telephone. The phone rings and that unmistakable voice on the other end says, 'He . . . llo, Phil, have you got a . . . minute?' Half an hour and a short accordion recital later, I am left with a broad grin on my face, a new tune in the bag and another hilarious story for an audience who by now are eagerly awaiting the next 'Fergie instalment'.

Aly Bain and I get as many requests for Fergie stories as we do for tunes. I have in the past described Fergie as a multi-faceted individual (even to look at!) – musician, hotelier, deer stalker, champion clay pigeon shot, fisherman . . . the list is endless. The thing is he brings his wonderful warm personality to everything he does and makes life a joy for all who encounter him. I can't wait to get my teeth into this book and arm myself with stories for the next tour!

Phil Cunningham
September 2003

Introduction

It was the year 1938 that saw Benny Goodman's band and quartet give the first ever performance of jazz music at Carnegie Hall. The province of New England was left counting the cost of the 'Long Island Express', one of the largest hurricanes ever recorded. A total of 8,900 homes and buildings had been destroyed, and over 60,000 people left homeless, as record winds ravaged the eastern seaboard of America.

Across the Atlantic, the Italian Enrico Fermi was presented with the Nobel Prize for physics, as a result of his demonstrations of the existence of new radioactive elements produced by irradiation, and for his related discovery of nuclear reactions brought about by slow neutrons. The same year also witnessed dramatic events on mainland Europe, as yet more countries fell in the face of the relentless *Blitzkrieg*. Other earth-shattering occurrences included the birth of one 'Duncan Ferguson MacDonald' (a.k.a. Fergie).

Scotland itself was a very different place in 1938. Thirteen million people had flocked to see the Empire Exhibition in Glasgow's Bellahouston Park. This was to be 'a celebration of the achievements of the British Empire', staged at a cost of £11,000,000 (an astronomical figure in those days). Looking back, it is hard to countenance such flamboyance, given Scotland's perilous state as a country tentatively drawing its first breaths after the worst rigours of the depression. Nevertheless, the May festival had proved a popular distraction for a population whose thoughts had turned once more to possible conflict with Germany. Opinion remained split over just how big a threat the Nazis posed.

In September of that year, Prime Minister Neville Chamberlain attempted to soothe any fears by returning with a written assurance from Herr Hitler that conflict could, and would be avoided. His 'Peace in our Time' speech, from Heston Airport, was one of the first to be televised and recorded by the BBC.

Incidentally, in 1938 a bottle of whisky would have cost you roughly fifteen shillings, and you could have bought fifty 'Players' cigarettes for two shillings and sixpence.

The district of Moidart, guarded by Loch Shiel to the south and the hills of Morar to the north, remained largely untouched by the affairs of that time (give or take the arrival of several thousand Allied troops in 1942). Life carried on as it always had done. The traditional industries of crofting and fishing were still strong, and were supplemented by seasonal employment on the large sporting estates in the area.

Gaelic, although actively discouraged by a disapproving education system, was still the language of choice for the 'Mùideartaich' (the Moidart People), and was to remain the dominant tongue up until the 1970s. The area remains, in mainland terms, a stronghold of Gaelic culture, and was always noted for its deference to music and the traditional arts. It is hardly surprising that a young aspiring musician was able to hone his talents in such an environment.

Fergie MacDonald was raised in a typical West Highland croft house, in a typically West Highland community. The crofting townships of Moidart were close-knit and cohesive. Collective effort formed the cornerstone of survival, and family ties ensured loyalty and respect for kith and kin. It was a secure and safe environment, where young and old were cared for in equal measure.

Moidart, in common with the rest of the Highlands, has, for centuries, been besieged by the problem of economic stagnation. The economy, which has been largely based on small-scale agriculture, has struggled to cope with the ever-changing demands of the modern world. This has facilitated the migration of countless thousands of young Highlanders, who have gravitated towards the industrial heartland of central Scotland, or have been seduced by the promise of wealth in the New World.

Twentieth-century Glasgow was, at various times, awash with Highland exiles, all of whom sought the chance to improve their lot in life. These people found employment in service and in nursing, in the shipyards, in mills and factories, and, most notably, in the city's police force. Scotland's universities too, were filled with Highland students, many of whom would go on to forge successful careers in various professions.

Like most immigrant populations, the Highlanders were fiercely territorial, settling in large swathes of Glasgow's west and south-west. Many neighbourhoods became almost Gaelic-speaking ghettos, as the northern tribes fought to assert their identity in the big smoke. New arrivals were welcomed into family homes, and were given assistance until able to stand on their own two feet.

The chord with the ancestral homeland was never severed, and this saw the emergence of numerous societies, each owing allegiance to a different area of the Highlands; the 'Lewis and Harris', the 'Glasgow Skye', the 'Sutherland', the 'Wester Ross' the 'South Uist and Barra'. These associations were initially formed with the express aim of improving the economic situation in the Highlands. As time progressed they began to fill an equally important social role within the city. Their various ceilidhs and dances became great focal points for Glasgow's Gaels. In many ways, Fergie MacDonald would become the doyen of this cultural subset.

Almost paradoxically, Fergie's prominence as a band-leader in Glasgow would ensure his place in the pantheon of Highland music, as news of his fame radiated back towards the homeland. It is the archetypal rags-to-riches story.

He is an iconic figure. Of this there can be no doubt. It could also be argued that he has worked hard at cultivating his image, living by the mantra that 'any publicity is good publicity'. Who could blame him? After all, our culture is that bit richer for his existence. Stories of his exploits have become legion, and one can easily envisage a day where the 'Fergie Story' will become the Highland equivalent of English folklore's 'Jack Tale'.

Fergie MacDonald, now in his sixty-fifth year, stands alone as testament to an age of unparalleled change in Scotland. He remains constant in his beliefs and values, and indefatigable in his work as a musician. The last great dance-band leader? It is a moot point. What cannot be debated is his popularity and place in the hearts and minds of his public. Generations have danced, laughed, cried and fallen in love to his sound, and this shows no sign of abating.

Iconoclastic, perverse, outrageous, warm; he is all of these things and more. Phil Cunningham, that virtuoso master of the accordion, once described Fergie as 'multi-faceted, even to look at'. It is a fitting depiction.

Incidentally, you can no longer buy a bottle of whisky for fifteen shillings, or fifty 'Players' cigarettes for two shillings and sixpence, well, not in the Clanranald Hotel anyway.

1
Early Days

My father and mother were married in 1932. Three years later, in 1935, Mum was expecting her first baby, and because we lived in such an isolated part of the world, the local doctor decided that it would be safe enough to have the birth at home. However, things did not go smoothly at all. Her labour started and lasted for the best part of a week. My mother had the most horrific time altogether.

The baby, a little girl, was still-born. It had been a horrendous experience. The doctor and the nurses had done everything they possibly could, but to no avail. It was a very sad time indeed in my mother's life.

In 1938, my mother was once more expecting, and it was decided early on that she would be taken to Rotten Row Hospital in Glasgow. Mother was taken away, and that is where I was born. To avoid further unnecessary complications, I was delivered by Caesarean section. That made things very, very much easier for my poor mother, and for the baby, who was myself.

One might say that I was born a Glaswegian. There is nothing wrong with that, but sometimes when I am filling out forms these days, folk find my place of birth rather strange, as I have been associated with the West Highlands of Scotland all my life. Anyway, that was the birth of Duncan Ferguson MacDonald in 1938.

The gentleman from whom I took my name was also the gentleman that we have to thank for getting my mother away so promptly, and for making life so much easier for her. He was the local doctor, Duncan Ferguson, a most wonderful man. He had been the victim of a mustard-gas attack during the First World War, and to be very honest, he was often tending patients who weren't half as ill as himself. My mother thought so highly of him (as did everyone in the locality) that she decided to call me after him.

A year after my birth, hostilities began once more with Germany, so technically I was a war baby. My first years were spent knowing nothing but war, and I still have vivid memories of the war reaching its peak, and how it effected us all in Moidart, as I would have been about five or six years old.

Much of Moidart was cordoned of as a training area for special forces. Many thousands of Allied troops must have been put through their paces on our uniquely rugged terrain. One intake would appear one week, and then be gone the next, off to occupied France or the Low Countries. Nobody could be sure. That is how it was for the duration of the war. Landing craft in Kentra Bay, route marches and assault courses became a part of everyday life.

I remember so well the mock battles that they used to have at night. The whole of the area used to be lit up with flares and 'tracers'. All night long you could hear the constant crackle of machine-guns and the thud of mortars. That is really what I was brought up with.

It is amazing also when I think of the toys that we used to play with as children. The place was littered with every sort of weaponry that one can think of: bullets and mortars, live and spent. We used to come across ranges and dumps where the commandos were firing off rounds. Amongst these spent bullets we used to find a lot of live rounds; .303 Sten Gun bullets, Bren Gun rounds. There were even .22 bullets, which must have been used as a lead-on to the bigger rifles.

All our games were influenced by the military presence around us; 'soldiers' and leaping from the highest rock we could find, to simulate the parachute jumps being carried out by the commandos. Worst of all, we discovered that if you hit the bottom of a bullet with a heavy rock, it would detonate. During our lunch-hour and playtimes we would amuse ourselves by setting off .303 bullets. How we weren't killed I will never know. Mills bombs, grenades, mortars – we had them all. We used to keep them in our very own secret arms dump that nobody else knew about. When I think about it now, it is really quite frightening. I would be terrified of children playing with such articles these days. Back then it was just part of the game; we never thought of the dangers.

I can also remember hearing the Nazi propaganda broadcasts by 'Lord Haw Haw' on the radio, firing out his ideals at us all. I don't suppose I was terribly aware of what propaganda was, but I was certainly aware of his voice. I can remember everyone imitating him. How the Germans thought that such a plummy English accent would win over the people of the Highlands is beyond me. Despite the war, it was a happy time – one full of adventures for a small boy. It was not until after the war however, that my interest in music was aroused.

The year was 1952. The well-known Dundee music shop 'J.T. Forbes' used to advertise accordions in the *Oban Times*, which my mother, Mima, bought faithfully every Thursday. My father, John, sent to J.T. Forbes for the catalogue. After much discussion, and working out of the financial aspects, we sent away for an accordion. It was a forty-eight bass piano accordion, costing £8 10s, payable at ten shillings per month.

There was nobody in the district who could teach music in any shape or form. Therefore by Christmas 1952, after months of hard work, my repertoire consisted of three tunes, all played on the black notes. My favourite tunes were 'Oh come all ye faithful' and 'Sugar bush, I love you so'.

Every year, the little village hall in Mingarry held the annual 'Night of the Three Kings' dance, in early January. Music was provided by the Roshven Ceilidh Band. They were a Gaelic-speaking group of shepherds, who played ceilidh music in its truest sense. Peggy MacRae played the drums, with brothers Donald and Dougie on the fiddle and younger brother Farquhar on the two-row button accordion. Other members outside the family included Aonghas Grant, Simon MacKinnon, Iain MacKinnon, Walter Begg and Alec Richardson. Although the music in general was good, my own ear was tuned into the button box. I used to sit beside the stage all night listening to Farquhar MacRae playing his button-key melodeon.

Hall ceilidhs and dances were a pretty regular occurrence in Moidart at that time, and the tradition of 'ceilidhing' in people's houses was still strong in the area. The ceilidhs held in the Mingarry and Shielbridge halls were magical occasions for a young boy like me, and I remember them fondly.

There would be anything up to twenty-five different singers and instrumentalists at each ceilidh, all of whom were very talented. I will always remember a gentleman, a very fine singer and fiddle player, who used to dance the 'Highland fling' on the stage, with his shoes off and his trousers tucked in at the ankles with bicycle clips – Roddy MacDonald, 'Langal'. Roddy is still living at the ripe old age of eighty-two, and was the last ploughman that I remember in the Moidart area. You used to see him walking his two horses every morning and every night to plough the local fields. A great guy and a wonderful character.

The list of Gaelic singers at these ceilidhs would be endless: Donald Cameron, 'the Post Office', Donald Cameron, 'Raelands', who had a most amazing voice. He growled all the time; there was no tonal quality to his voice whatsoever. Where he captured the audience was with his humorous songs. They didn't need any musical embellishments. My own mother, Mima MacDonald, would sing; Sheila Dewar, Archie MacNaughton 'the butcher', Iain Smith, 'Kinlochmoidart' and many more. May MacKinnon and Archie Manuel would play the fiddle, Dr Frank Davidson and Geordie Watt would play the accordion and John Johnstone, from Shielfoot, Charlie MacLean and Duncan Henderson would play the pipes. All three were wonderful pipers, and they would be joined by Allan MacDonald from Dorlin (Ailean Ailean) who thought he could play the pipes, and gave some hilarious performances as a result. One night, his pipes weren't going all that well, and one of the other pipers offered to have a quick look at them. He gave one of the drones a quick blow and several reeds came flying out from the top of it. The pipes were giving off the most terrible squeaks and yelps, and a local wit, Allan MacNeil, said 'stand back folks, she's going to have more kittens yet'.

The master of ceremonies or '*Fear an Taighe*' at most of these wonderful ceilidhs would be Alec Dan Henderson from Newton or Alasdair Cameron, better known to us all as 'North Argyll'. They were wonderful fun.

You are dealing here also with the cream of the local indigenous talent. The best people in the world probably. The halls used to be packed out on ceilidh night. I remember we used to go to the Acharacle ceilidhs, walking there and back with my mother and father.

After the war, we had 'pictures' in the hall, once a fortnight. This entertainment was run by the Highlands and Islands Film Guild. This used to be a laugh as well, you know. I wasn't very old, but I was certainly aware of what was going on around me. A lot of the men and the young fellows would have half-bottles with them, going to 'the pictures'. Their voices would get louder as the night went on, and all you would hear would be 'shh, be quiet' and 'shut up Lachie John' all around you. In the end you wouldn't be able to hear what was going on in the film for the riot that would be going on around you. Then the man in charge of the projector would switch on all the lights, and threaten everybody that if peace and quiet were not restored he would pack up and go home. I remember one night when things got a wee bit heated, and a fight started in the back seats. The boys were thumping hell out of each other.

Roddy MacDonald, 'Langal's' father, had a lorry, and he used to collect everyone in the area and take them over to the hall in Acharacle. The lorry would be chock-a-block with folk, old folk as well. People would be lifted into the back of the lorry like stags or hinds. That was amazing too.

Local dances were also incredibly popular, and were an occasion in their own right. That was the era of the carryout, which would be plonked somewhere outside the hall. You had your half-bottles and your 'screw tops', which you weren't allowed to take into the hall, so you had to hide them somewhere in the hall environs. There were no plastic bags in those days. You arrived with a half-bottle 'on the hip' and your pockets full of 'screw tops'. The trick was to find a wall or a bush behind which you might hide your carryout.

Whenever a particular dance finished, there would be a lull, as all the men disappeared outside for a crack at the carryout. After a while, it didn't matter very much whether you hit your own carryout or not. More often than not, it was so dark that you knew roughly where it was, but there would be many others stashed there as well. You would be swigging away with your friends, back in for a couple of dances and back out for another swig. That was the way of it.

There was always the inevitable fight, usually over a girl, although it was also a good place for sorting out local feuds: crofters fighting over livestock and land. You would meet your adversary at the dance and hopefully knock spots off him. Fights were very chivalrous affairs in those days. These days you would clonk the guy before he had an opportunity to blink, but in those days you always challenged the guy first of all. You had time to take off your jacket, roll up your sleeves, take your tie off and square up, outside of course, and that was it. Off the fight would go. What I used to love was the women getting involved in all these fights. There would be about fifteen women screaming and trying to hold the fighters back. This was the scene. It usually turned out that there would be no fight worth seeing, because the women would be getting in the way. The two warrior braves would be shouting all kinds of obscenities and challenges, without ever really getting to grips with one another. After the excitement was over, everyone would pile back into the hall and the dance would really start. Dances never finished before four o'clock in the morning. That was the normal time for finishing.

The rota for dancing was 'Quadrilles', 'Lancers', 'Eightsome Reel', 'Circassion Circle' and 'Petronella'. Real hard set dancing, and this went on all night long. There would be at least six shots at the 'Quadrilles' and the same for the 'Lancers'. It was a marathon. The standard of dancing was so high as well. Everyone knew these dances and everyone was able to dance, and dance well.

At all these dances, there would always be a tea, and this was the highlight of the night. It would always happen about one in the morning. An old tub loaded with cups would be taken round the hall, and everyone would take one. This would be followed by women who went round with these huge urns full of tea and with jugs of milk and sugar. Then tray after tray of sandwiches, cakes, scones and pancakes would be carried round the hall. That, in my book, was Highland culture at its very best.

It grieves me terribly that this has been lost. Recently, there was a good-going ceilidh band and two or three top-line Gaelic singers appearing in the local hall. There were eighteen people at that ceilidh. The following week there was a string quartet in the hall, giving a recital of classical music, and the place was packed. How times have changed.

During the long winter nights, one of our local worthies, Lachie John MacEachan, would arrive at our little croft house. He would set off from his house in Dorlin with his melodeon strapped on his back, with no case, in the pouring rain. The bellows would be saturated, with amazing sounds coming from the keys. Nevertheless, I soon found that I was making much more progress with Lachie John's old button box than with my own piano accordion. It was back to J.T. Forbes in Dundee. The piano accordion was returned and exchanged for a two-row Hohner, 'Black Dot' button box. The price was £15, and again, my father, John, paid for it in monthly instalments of ten shillings.

A Saturday night in this remote part of the Highlands consisted, in those days, of radio entertainment, of which the highlight was the BBC programme of Scottish dance music. In a short period of time, favorite band sounds were established like 'Jimmy Shand', 'Bobby MacLeod', 'Alistair Downie', 'Jim Cameron', 'the Wick Scottish Dance Band' and the 'Hawthorn Accordion Band', amongst many others. Again, there being no one in the area to give any tips whatsoever, all my tunes were played in the key of C. At least it made one develop one's own particular style.

The problem of learning tunes was a major drawback. This was overcome by purchasing an 'His Master's Voice' gramophone. It had to be wound up by hand, and a new needle lasted, usually, for one night. The first tune I learned by this method was the 'Balmoral Highlanders', played by Bobby MacLeod. I have often wondered how many needles were used, how many times the handle was birled round, and how many times the six parts of the 'Balmoral Highlanders' were played before I learnt the tune. Many of the notes were difficult to grasp, but luckily great help was given to me by a young piper from the area, previously mentioned, Charlie MacLean. He was of tremendous help to me, with the phrasings and the grace notes.

During this period, I was attending Fort William High School. My friends in fifth and sixth year were all from the Hebrides. We used to spend all our spare time in Marion Weir's music shop, listening to Scottish dance music records. The weekly pocket-money was always spent on the most recent '78' released. I remember the most popular names at that time, in the mid-50s, were Will Starr, Bobby MacLeod and Jimmy Shand. The hit tunes were 'The Jacqueline Waltz', 'The Bluebell Polka' and 'Murdo MacKenzie of Torridon'.

By this time I had discovered a button-box bandleader in Fort William called Jimmy MacGillivray. Jimmy taught me the scales of A, D and G, but would not or could not teach me anything further, as he himself could not read music. To this day, I maintain that a button-box player should first be shown the scales. From there on, they should be left to develop their own particular style and technique. If not, they will find themselves playing like 5,000 more box players in Scotland, without any individual skills whatsoever.

Around this time I had an unfortunate experience, which was to have a profound effect on my school career. While staying at the Green Hill Hostel in Fort William, I contracted conjunctivitis. I got up one morning, with both eyes tightly shut, and discharging matter. I eventually managed to open them, to find that the whites of the eyes were red raw. I thought that it might have been caused by a draught or something, but the matron, Miss MacDonald, sent me down to the doctor's surgery straight away.

I well remember that the doctor on duty that day was Doctor MacIvor. He took a look at my eyes and knew right away what the problem was. He informed me that I had conjunctivitis, but that he could sort it, no problem whatsoever. He gave me ointment, and I continued with that treatment for about a week. However, this didn't seem to work. There was no sign of the infection clearing up, so back I went to the doctor, who gave me drops to try. After another week with no significant improvement, the doctor signed me off school, for I wasn't able to take part in any lessons or exams, or anything. I was sent home – back to Moidart.

On my arrival home, I came under the care of our own local doctor, my namesake, Duncan Ferguson, who recommended a change in medication. The problem continued for weeks and weeks though, without any sign of change or improvement. It was then decided that I should be referred to a specialist in Glasgow.

To cut a long story short, this went on for nearly one year, and I missed out on a lot of schooling, finding myself a year behind my contemporaries. I continued on the same medication for almost a whole year. Nothing seemed to change. I thought I would never recover, until one morning I awoke to find the condition completely cleared. It was amazing. Various specialists and doctors wondered and speculated as to how this could have happened. Nobody knew. I had tried so many different treatments and medications. All to no avail: and then suddenly, for no apparent reason, I was cured.

Having said that, it has certainly left its mark. I have had very tender eyes ever since. If I am out on the hill, in any kind of wind, my eyes water severely, and are very sensitive to most things.

When I look back on that period now, I realise that although I lost a year's schooling, I gained an awful lot in return, because it was during that period that I got heavily into the accordion for the first time. The amount of time I spent at home was put to good use, and I began honing my talents and learning the rudiments which would stand me in good stead in the years to come.

By the time I finished at Fort William High School, I could manage a number of marches, jigs, reels and waltzes, all in the correct keys, all played entirely by ear. The highlight of my sixth year at school was the night that six of us, all from Green Hill Hostel, decided to climb out on the fire escape at midnight, to hear Bobby MacLeod playing in the Highland Hotel. The first person we saw at the dance was Johnny Walker, our English master. Finally, to round off a wonderful evening, the boys who didn't go to the dance pulled up the fire-escape rope while we were away. Here we were, standing outside the hostel at three o'clock in the morning, with our best suits on, and not daring to ring the main doorbell. Expulsion would have been the name of the game. Finally, after many stones had been hurled at a particular friendly bedroom window, a welcome face appeared and lowered the fire-escape rope. To his eternal credit, Johnny Walker remained a silent witness to this amazing escapade; and if I remember correctly, he even bought us a beer!

One of my earliest memories of playing at a dance was when I was sixteen years of age. I was still a pupil at Fort William Senior Secondary School. Farquhar MacRae – who became one of my dearest and closest friends – phoned and asked if I would play at a dance in Glenuig on the following Friday night. Farquhar, his brothers and other noted local musicians played at almost every dance in the Moidart area at this time. They were known as the Roshven band, and to be asked to play with them was a great honour.

In those days, I always had a haversack, a green, ex-army haversack, in which I carried my accordion. On the Friday afternoon, my accordion on my back, I made for Fort William train station, and caught the 4.30 train to Lochailort. I will always remember Farquhar waiting for me on the platform at Lochailort, a strong, fit young man. We walked the mile or so to Farquhar's house, where his mother had bacon and eggs waiting for us.

In the early evening we made our way down to the jetty, where Ronald MacDonald – the 'Whaler' as he was known affectionately, on account of his time spent on the whaling ships in South Georgia – was waiting for us aboard his launch the *Jacobite*. In those days there was no road further than Lochailort, so the boat was a necessity. We were soon joined by a crowd of revellers all going to the dance, and we set sail for Glenuig.

I remember the trip down the loch so well. It was a beautiful summer's evening in June. The sun was starting to set behind the small isles of Rum and Eigg. Everyone would have a carryout, maybe a half-bottle and a couple of bottles of beer, or 'screw tops' as we called them. I was at an age where I had started to experiment with taking a wee smoke and a dram, and soon we started making music. The ceilidh was in full swing onboard the *Jacobite* when we arrived at the small pier at Samalaman.

The dance was held in the old boathouse, which still stands to this day (though it is no longer used as a dance hall, as Glenuig now has its own purpose-built community centre). The band was: Dougie MacRae (Farquhar's older brother) on fiddle; a man called Alec Richardson, on drums; Walter Begg, who was the station-master at Lochailort, also on fiddle; and Farquhar and me on accordions. It must have gone on all night long. And the dancing . . . there were schottisches, quadrilles, eightsome reels, the lancers: you name it. Some of the finest dancers I ever saw, for it was a way of life in those days. The dance went on so long that the boat back to Lochailort ended up missing the tide at Samalaman, and had to tie up, instead, at the old Glenuig pier.

I remember (and it's funny when you think about it now) falling madly in love with a young girl at the dance, and afterwards, walking her back to the boat, where she departed. I, sadly, did not rejoin the boat as I was heading back towards Acharacle and home. I teamed up with maybe forty or fifty other young people as we headed over what was known as the 'Bridal Path' (a rough mountain track travelled on foot before the road was built). This was when the real operations started. Many of my travelling companions had secreted bottles of beer along the route on the way to the dance. This was so you wouldn't be getting a terrible drouth on the way home. Maybe a couple of bottles at one spot, and then, a few hundred yards on, another couple. This made the two or three miles over to Kinacarra all the more bearable.

On reaching Kinacarra, everyone climbed into (or onto) the various vehicles, which had been left there the night before, and after bidding each other goodnight or good morning, continued their journeys to Acharacle and beyond. I remember so well getting a ride home on the pillion of a Norton trials motorcycle. The early morning was as beautiful and as clear as the night before had been.

2
Highland Games

By the age of seventeen I was completing my sixth year at Fort William Senior Secondary School. I was still resident at the Green Hill Hostel, which was next to the High School in Achintore Road. Apart from playing the accordion, my other hobbies included football, shinty and athletics.

Athletics began to play a major part in life around this time, mainly due to the influence of Tommy MacEachan from Arasaig, who later in life became one of our top 'heavyweights' on the Highland games circuit, and Hamish Simpson from Mallaig, who became one of the top sprinters. Hamish later became Professor Simpson in the field of paediatrics.

Up to the age of eighteen my summers were devoted to competing at the various Highland games in the area. It becomes almost like a drug after a while. There is something about the sound of the bagpipes, the sight of Highland dancers and the smell of newly-cut grass, mingled with the aroma of 'Olive Oil, Winter Green Embrocation'.

The competition was fearsome, but sometimes hilarious. I remember a certain competitor in the pole vault, of all things. The pole had a spike at the end of it, like a cavalry lance, and 'Jimmy' used to charge down the track, ready for take off, dressed in a 'J.D. Williams' vest, underpants, with black socks, held up with suspenders, and no footwear at all.

One of the top meetings on the circuit was the Mull Highland games. I remember cycling from Acharacle to Lochaline, in Morvern. This took up most of the day, and after staying the night with relations, Johnny and Mary Ann Scoular, I caught the MacBrayne's steamer, the

Lochearn, from Lochaline to Tobermory. The *King George* sailed direct from Oban, and on board were perhaps 1,000 passengers, plus all the top athletes of the day and the City of Glasgow Police Pipe Band.

When we arrived in Tobermory, the *King George* had already docked, and the pipe band were playing selections along the waterfront, en route to the games field. It was a sight that I will never forget, and to this day I can vividly recall the enormous stature of one of the pipers, 'big Ronnie Lawrie', from Oban.

Then it was 'to the games'. There were four main sections at all Highland games: Highland dancing, piping, athletics and the heavy events. Around the 1955 period, the big names on the circuit were, from Highland dancing: Betty Jessiman, Jean Reynolds, Catriona Buchanan, May Falconer, Mary Godsman and Marjory MacDonald, Arasaig; in piping: Pipe Major Donald MacLeod, Donald MacLean, John Burgess and the MacFadyen brothers; in the 'heavy events', one had such names as Louis Stewart, Sandy Sutherland and Bill Anderson, who was just coming into things. The track events were dominated by the likes of Jay Scott and his brother Tom Scott, Willie Findlay, Gordon Grant, our own Farquhar and Dougie MacRae, Donald Black, from Lismore, Johnny MacDonald, from Dervaig, Lachie MacFadyen and the MacIntyres, MacIvors, and MacLeans from Tobermory.

One of my big disappointments in life is that I never managed to win the 'Chieftain's Cup', at Tobermory. The nearest I ever got was runner-up, just pipped at the post by Gordon Grant of Iona. That day, I picked up seven prizes, which I still have to this day. The list is really amazing, when one considers that nowadays most athletes channel their efforts into one event. My collection for that particular day was: (1) 100 yds, 3rd; (2) 220 yds, 3rd; (3) 440 yds, 3rd; (4) Long Jump, 2nd; (5) Hop, Step and Jump, 2nd; (6) Pole Vault, 2nd; (7) High Jump, 1st.

I remember going to the games-night dance at the Aros Hall in Tobermory. The band was Andrew Rankine's, and the hall was packed to capacity. It's funny, but all I remember about the band is Andrew Rankine himself, singing 'Roll Out the Barrel', for a Boston Two Step. When the dance was over I slept under a rock in Tobermory Bay, and caught the first ferry over to Kilchoan in the morning. The ferry was a little MacBrayne's boat called the *Loch Buie*, where I had my very first meeting with Henry MacMillan!

Henry, whom I got to know so well in later life, was a living legend. He was a remarkable character, considering that he was severely handicapped in the lower limbs. It added, however, to his outstanding personality. He always made sure, when you were going to dances and such like, that you had what he termed 'sporting tackle'. That is 'French letters' (or condoms) in everyday language.

Anyway, my destination was Kilchoan, and the 'West Ardnamurchan Sports and Regatta'. That was a good day for me on the games field, taking the gold medal for top athlete. The bag that day was five firsts, one second and two thirds. The top heavy that day was Douglas MacMillan, who later became Professor MacMillan and Moderator of the Free Church of Scotland.

At night, again, the games-night dance, which went on until three o'clock in the morning. The highlight of the evening was getting a lift back home to Acharacle with Donnie MacColl, a budding accordionist of my own age. Donnie had a brand new Renault Dauphine, which he smacked, side-on, into a hind at Glenborrodale. Luckily there was little damage to the car, and we celebrated with a swig out of Donnie's half-bottle.

Once I was home safely, it was a case of training every day, in preparation for the next games, which were usually on Saturdays. Highland games that I visited at that time included Inverary, Tobermory, Kilchoan, Morvern, Morar, Arasaig, Portree, Fort William, Roy Bridge, Aberlour and Glenfinnan.

During that summer of 1955, which was my final year at Fort William High School, I ventured out to the Hebrides for the first time in my life. The attraction was the South Uist Highland Games. The boat sailed from Mallaig the day before the games, and we had gale-force winds all the way. The *Lochmore* was packed to capacity with Uist people going home for the Glasgow Fair. Among the passengers were the Cameron Highlanders Territorials, going on their annual camp. The boat was full of musicians also, mainly pipers, who took it in turns to play selections. I haven't heard a bad piper yet from Uist. But what really took my fancy were two accordion players, both belting out marches, reels and jigs, in the bar. At that time I didn't know who they were but later I found out that their names were Jimmy Smith and Dickie Murray, both from Fort William, and both in the 4th/5th Camerons. I thoroughly enjoyed the music until the *Lochmore* was past Skye, and entered the Minch. The next three hours were spent down in the bog, vomiting my guts out and wishing I were dead. I have never experienced such sea-sickness in my life.

On arrival in Loch Boisdale I was met by one of my old school friends, John Angus O'Henley. It soon became clear that I would have to be put straight to bed, to try and get me fit for the games the following day. For me the games were a disaster, finishing up with a third in the Pole Vault, after going all that way. Then something happened which probably changed my life for ever. The games-night dance was held in the gym, at Balivanich. The hall was packed to the rafters, and there, sitting on the stage, all on his own, was this wee fat guy playing a three-row button box. The dance floor was heaving, and the people dancing on it were jumping. 'Who's that guy?' I asked someone. 'Oh that's a guy called Iain MacLachlan.'

I didn't know it then, but this guy was going to be world famous, and would become one of my dearest friends, both musically and personally.

On arriving home from this disastrous trip I got stuck into more training and preparation for the Glenfinnan and Oban games. Alas, it was not to be. I never made it.

One day a brown envelope appeared through the post, with a green letter in it. The government had other plans for me.

3
Army Days

In August 1955, like all fit young boys of my age, I was called up to complete two years of compulsory National Service in the armed forces. I was carrying home a bag of peat on my back, when the local postman, Donald MacLean, handed me the green letter from the War Office. I was instructed to report to Blenheim Barracks, Aldershot.

I can remember leaving home on a beautiful autumn morning, and sailing up Loch Shiel, from Acharacle to Glenfinnan, on the steamer *Clanranald*. This was followed by the long train journey from Glenfinnan to Aldershot. My last contact with civilian life was having a dram with old John Moynihan, the stationmaster at Glenfinnan. On arrival at Aldershot I found myself amongst 500 other recruits. There were Jocks, Geordies, Taffs, Cockneys, Paddies, you name it; they were all there. I became '23175260 Private MacDonald'.

The drill sergeant was an old soldier nearing discharge, with two rows of ribbons. He turned out to be the filthiest, most foul-mouthed man in the British Army. All the boys were seventeen and eighteen years old, with 'plooks' and pimples, and very little carnal knowledge (if any). Sergeant Vickers drilled a very sound sex education into us, during square bashing. Every single order had a sexual undertone. Bayonet drill had possibly the best examples of this i.e. 'Get it up!', 'Slide it in!', 'Ram it home!', and so on. What a guy this was. Every morning he would bombard us with the gory details of his exploits with his poor wife, and the tricks he would get up to on a forty-eight-hour pass to London's Piccadilly 'red light' district. Eventually, after eight weeks' basic training, we all passed out, with Sergeant Vickers at the head of the parade.

After this initial period I was lucky enough to be sent on a physical instructor's course at Salisbury. It was one of my happiest times in the army. I was there in the middle of winter, and I always remember the assault course, as I nearly killed myself on it. There was a high beam which was just about the breadth of your foot. You had to walk over it, and I remember it being very frosty on the morning that I tried it. The inevitable happened, and I slipped off, landing very awkwardly, which kept me in the medical reception station for nearly a week, with a twisted ankle. Luckily I was able to get back on the course and complete it.

This lasted another eight weeks, and on gaining the 'Crossed Swords', I was sent back to my battalion in Aldershot as a qualified instructor. The nature of my work was trying to get new recruits fit. We went through intake after intake. They were all on eight weeks' basic training. You would get a new intake coming in, and then, after eight weeks, they would pass out and another new lot would come in.

They were very happy days indeed. In my gymnasium there were six physical training instructors, all corporals and lance corporals, and a sergeant in charge of us all from the Army Physical Training Corps. They're a unit in their own right within the army. We all got on very well, which helped to engender the feeling that we were one big happy family. Our favorite ploy was to climb onto the flat roof of the gymnasium and bask in the sun. We were all as brown as berries: what a suntan we had!

We had a lad with us who was a very fine boxer. In fact he was middleweight champion of Southern Command. We used to act as his seconds when he was fighting, either for the battalion, or for the Southern Command team. His name was Bill Hucklesby. I lost track of Bill after leaving the army, but happened to discover his whereabouts thirty years later, through the strangest of circumstances.

I had been out stalking one day, and returned to the house cold and soaking wet. I switched on the six o'clock news while I was changing, to find that there had been an IRA bombing in London. The police officer in charge of the investigation was asked to make a statement. The caption on the television gave his name as Bill Hucklesby, head of the Anti-Terrorist Unit at Scotland Yard. There he was. He had obviously worked himself all the way to the top.

In the morning I decided that I was going to phone him to see if he would remember me, and I got through to the headquarters of the Metropolitan Police, at Scotland Yard. I explained that I was Fergie MacDonald from the Highlands, and that I wanted to have a word with Bill Hucklesby. 'I'm afraid that's not possible,' said the voice at the other end. 'You would have to be checked out thoroughly before we could let you do that.' So he took down my name, address, my age, what I was doing etc. They obviously contacted the local police in Fort William to complete their checks.

Anyway, a fortnight later a letter arrived, and who was it from but the commander of the Anti-Terrorist Unit at Scotland Yard, Bill Hucklesby. He remembered me as 'Jock', the guy that used to keep him awake at night playing the accordion. It was wonderful to hear from him. It had been our first contact since we were nineteen-year-olds in the army.

It was after returning to Aldershot that my accordion arrived, through the post, from home. Clearly the box didn't rate very highly in my plans during these days. What I do remember very vividly during this period 1956–7 were the chart numbers in the top twenty. We used to dance the night away in the clubs and dives of Aldershot. The most popular numbers were 'Heartbreak Hotel' and 'You Load Sixteen Tons and What do You Get?' There was a strange way of dancing during this period. Foreheads were in contact, with both hands around your partner's bum. As the night went on, the music got slower, the beat got heavier, the lights got dimmer, and there was only a gentle swaying movement, from the couples dancing to the slow heavy beat. Sergeant Vickers' techniques, during drill instruction, suddenly started to pay dividends. However, by the time our two years were up, and we were ready for demob, most of us could teach even Sergeant Vickers a trick or two.

We had quite a lively social life, and would be out on the town most Saturday nights. On one particular Saturday we were all sitting about in our billet, when a dispatch rider arrived from another unit, dressed up in his leathers and helmet and goggles and all sorts of gear.

He asked where the HQ offices were, so we guided him over. He said he would also need a 'chit' for his billet and something to eat, and we said that we would sort that out for him. He must have been a lance corporal or something, because he returned to say that he had been given a bed with us. There were only seven or eight beds in our wee billet anyway. We had all planned to go out on the town, and we asked the dispatch rider if he wanted to come with us, but he didn't. 'I can't go dressed like this,' he said, what with his leather breeks and leather jerkins and all the other things that dispatch riders wore. 'No,' he said, 'I'll just wait in tonight boys and get a good night's sleep.' That was fine. We didn't really know the guy anyway, so we made our way down the town for a night of revelry, and we had our usual debauched Saturday night in the dives of Aldershot.

We returned to camp in the early hours of the morning, to find an awful upheaval. The place was flooded with military police and duty officers. Our billet was overrun with uniforms wanting to take down names and details, wondering if anyone had seen anything, or wished to make a statement.

Eventually we found out what had happened. We had another filthy old sergeant, by the name of Feeney, who had been in the army for years and years. He had joined before the Second World War, and had served in the Far East and the Middle East, and had obviously become warped by the sun and whisky and women. Sergeant Feeney must have fancied the dispatch rider, with all his leathers on. He must have got some kind of kick out of it, because he jumped into bed and tried to molest him. He must have taken him by surprise, and tried to do the dirty on him.

The dispatch rider leapt out of bed and ran over (in his shorts probably) to the guard room. Before you knew it, the duty officer was there, military police, the whole shooting match. Poor old Sergeant Feeney was whipped away and charged. Whether he got a stretch in Colchester or not, I'm not all that sure, but it certainly created a great laugh for us when we came back from our night out. It was probably the highlight of our night. We just regarded it as great *craic*.

If there are any ex-army men reading this, they will know straight away what Colchester meant. That was the military prison. If you went to Colchester, you would most certainly come out a broken man. It was a byword for torture; running up and down sand dunes all day with a full pack on, amongst other horrors. The military police in Colchester were just the worst form of humanity imaginable. They were hand picked from the scum of the earth, and in many ways were worse than the prisoners. If you were sent to Colchester, your life would never be the same again. Luckily, I never came close to being sent there, and my time in the army continued as enjoyably as ever. But finally the big day arrived: '23175260 Corporal MacDonald' was demobbed and on his way back to Moidart.

4
A Year in the Wilderness

I returned from national service in September 1958, by which time my mind was focused on a medical career. Physiotherapy was the choice. The immediate problem was that I had failed chemistry and physics while at Fort William High School. Anyhow, I applied for a physiotherapy degree course, starting in October 1959. I was accepted, pending my passing in chemistry and physics at the Scottish Education Preliminary Examinations. Fortunately, after swotting all winter, I eventually passed both of them in March 1959.

The winter of 1958–9 was probably one of the happiest periods of my life. Swotting for my two Highers, poaching and playing the box. I am not ashamed of my poaching exploits. It was purely for the pot and friendly neighbours. The technique was to dismantle the shotgun, in order to hide the butt and barrel separately beneath one's jacket. When a stag or hind was stalked, you then assembled the twelve-bore gun, and you used a home-made cartridge. This cartridge was loaded with five deadly lead balls. At thirty yards, this was lethal. The deer would be shot, carried home at night, skinned and eaten, either fresh or salted. There were many close shaves, but luckily I was never caught.

The accordion came very much into things then. At night, mother would have on these 'roasters' of fires, and I would be learning new tunes for hours on end, every night. In those days every musician was brainwashed into believing that there was no other music but Scottish country-dance music. Therefore the type of tunes one learned were 'Hamilton House', 'Machine Without Horses', 'Scottish Reform', 'Cumberland Reel', etc.

I formed my first band in the summer of 1958, with drums, accordion and bass. The bass instrument was a big tea chest, with a large round hole cut out of one side. A brush handle was hammered onto the other side, and thick fishing gut was the only string.

During the day I had a job with Balfour Kilpatrick of Paisley, digging holes for a new hydro line. One of my work-mates was Wee Archie from Glasgow, who played the drums. He would go home to Glasgow once a month, and on his return he would tell us all (at the tea break) how he used to throw his wage packet on the floor the moment he walked into his house. His poor wife would bend down to pick it up, and he would immediately mount her from behind. His stories were hilarious during these tea breaks. Eventually, we had a further addition to our band, in the form of a washing board. You see, 'skiffle' was pretty big then, and we were into Lonnie Donegan's music in a big way. For a 'Strip the Willow', one could adapt 'skiffle' numbers like 'Last Train to San Fernando' and 'Does Your Chewing Gum Lose its Flavour on the Bed Post Overnight'.

We all saved up and bought an amplifier and two speakers for the sum of £2. I remember the lead connecting to the microphone was kept in place by two matches pushed into the positive and negative terminals. My first band engagement was in Ardtornish Hall, Morvern. We hired a car to take us there and back. By the time we had paid Allan MacDonald (Allan Kinicarra) £2 10s, we had £2 10s left for ourselves. We all got ten shillings each. To crown it all, the amplifier began to throw out blue smoke, and eventually burst into flames. The hall-keeper, Sammy Hendry, threw buckets of sand over the poor amplifier, as the hall was all wood. The only protection against fire that halls had in those days was a bucket of sand. He was obviously scared that the whole place would go up. What an end to my first engagement!

There were a lot of local dances during that summer, though most of the time there was no payment. The band would maybe swell to ten musicians on the stage, in the early part of the night. By the early hours of the morning the dancers would come to a sudden stop, as all the musicians were either indulging in a touch of *Baile Cnocan*, or polishing off half-bottles in cars parked outside the hall. Eventually a few musicians would be flushed out of the cars, and the dance would get going again. That was the way it was.

Gaelic songs were always used for waltzes, and it was wonderful to hear everyone singing with the band. I would say that 95 per cent of the dancers would have spoken Gaelic in those days.

The final engagement with this beautiful little band before I moved to Glasgow, was performing at the end of the season in the big house on Eilean Shona. There was a launch which brought everyone from the jetty at Dorlin, on the mainland, to this amazing dance. The hostess, Lady Howard de Walden, would not allow alcohol at these annual balls. The event reminds me now of the film *Whisky Galore*. The drink was hidden in perfume bottles, lemonade bottles, thermos flasks, etc. As there was no way of gauging how much one had consumed, while having a sudden gulp behind a tree or a shed, the results were devastating. The band ended up paralytic, along with the guests. The piper, old Donald Kennedy, who had no teeth at all, employed a young boy to hold the blow stick of the bagpipe in his mouth, as it kept slipping out of Donald's. Isn't that just beautiful? The climax of the event was the launch ending up high and dry on a sand bank, at four o'clock in the morning. We were stranded there until eight o'clock, when the tide came back in. I remember playing the box to help flagging morale during that imposed stay on our desert island.

I now believe that that was my basic grounding in the world of real ceilidh music and ceilidh band culture. The modern conception of the terminology 'ceilidh band' and 'ceilidh music' leaves me utterly sick. One could say that there is no cultural link-up these days.

5
Fergie Hits Glasgow

On arrival in Glasgow, in October 1959, 'digs' were set up in Belmont Street, with Mary MacDonald of Keppoch, Roy Bridge. I also attended my first lectures in anatomy and physiology at the Anderson College of Medicine. I had started a four-year course of physiotherapy, leading to the MFPh degree, which seemed a million years away. During the first week I also joined the Glasgow University Ossianic Society. In 1959 the Ossianic Society was comprised entirely of Gaelic-speaking Highland students. The president when I enrolled was Neil Fraser, from Skye, who many years later became head of BBC Scotland.

At that time, the Ossianic Society had no fewer than four mod gold medallists in its membership: Alasdair Gillies, Kenna Campbell, Alma Kerr and Calum Ross. You can imagine the fantastic ceilidh nights we all participated in on Friday nights, at the Queen Margaret Union, our meeting place. I even got my name in the syllabus as a committee member. My official title was 'Ceilidh Accordionist'. Eventually, after four years, the society made me an honorary member, for services rendered. The citation read more like a list of battle honours; 'The Edinburgh Annual', 'Tours of the Hebrides', 'The Annual Picnic to Aberfoyle', to name but a few.

Two of my fondest memories of these wonderful years are from the infamous 'Ossianic tour of Skye and Lewis' in 1960. The first was my introduction to 'bothans' (illegal drinking dens), after a ceilidh in Shawbost Hall, on the Island of Lewis. The second was my first experience of *Danns an Rathad* (a road dance) at 'Sluggan's Bridge', following a ceilidh in Portree. Talk about battle honours. Waterloo had nothing on this little lot!

The night in Portree was incredible. Somebody (I don't remember who) suggested that we go to 'Sluggan's Bridge' for our own version of the *Danns an Rathad*. It was a great idea, apart from the fact that I ended up carrying my accordion all the way there, and it must be some distance outside Portree. This, of course, was coupled with the inevitable carryouts that we had with us. It turned out to be a most eventful route march, with halts here and there for a refreshment and a quick rehearsal for the 'Sluggan's Bridge' road dance. I remember playing for an eightsome reel after we arrived, and then everyone did a Highland schottische.

We all returned then to Mrs Urquhart's famous Caley Hotel in Portree. I was staying in a room with five other boys who had also just finished their national service. We were still full of all the mannerisms and jargon from our army days. I remember so well my dear friend, Calum Ross, who had been a sergeant, telling us to stand by our beds at six o'clock in the morning. He carried out a mock inspection of us all and gave Corporal MacDonald an awful bollocking altogether for some reason or other.

Eventually, we left the Isle of Skye and headed for our next port of call, Lewis, where we had a night in Stornoway Town Hall. This was a concert followed by a dance. We were all playing at the concert, but I remember that we did not play for the dance. That duty was left to a local group who called themselves 'The Stornoway Dance Band'. That was my first meeting with the late Iain Crichton, a wonderful musician and composer. He was a young fellow then, playing his five-row continental button box. They were a very good band.

The next night found us in Shawbost Hall, and this occasioned my first experience of 'bothans', or illegal drinking dens, as I mentioned earlier. It is a night that I will remember for the rest of my life. We arrived to find the place heaving with people. We performed the concert with the usual programme of music and song and a play led by Murdo Beaton and John Finlayson, which went down a storm.

As was the custom all over the Highlands at that time, the ceilidh would finish and everybody would leave the hall until the chairs had been cleared. Whereupon, everyone would come back in, pay their money for the dance, and the night would start again. While all this was going on, a young man who is now head of the Harris Tweed industry, Derek Murray, asked a few of the musicians if we would like a dram. We indicated that we would, and he told us to follow him. We thought that we would be going out to a car for a quick pull at a half-bottle, but that notion was soon dispelled when we by-passed the car park completely, following a fairly precarious footpath. It was then that I set my eyes on the Shawbost bothan for the first time. I didn't know what to make of it. It was a small corrugated-iron building with a thatched roof and a chimney. The scene inside the bothan is one that I will never forget. The stove was white with the heat from a roaring peat fire, and the whisky was flowing like a river in spate. Not only that, but the place was mobbed.

After a number of drams we decided that we'd better head back and get on with the dance. Luckily I had had the sense to realise that I was responsible for the music on that particular night and had taken it relatively easy. It was a good job, as when half-time arrived, and the rest of the band trooped off for a cup of tea, I was dragged back to the bothan, which was really starting to come to life. In fact the bothan never really reached its peak of activity until the dance finished at four o'clock in the morning. What amazing stamina the people of Shawbost had!

That was my first real taste of touring in the islands. It was an experience which I enjoyed very much, and one that I have repeated on numerous occasions since those happy days. The Ossianic tour was a huge success, and we all eventually returned to Glasgow in fine fettle, having cemented our various friendships.

During this period, I was beginning to out-grow my two-row button box. Every Saturday afternoon my student pals and I would congregate at the 'Curlers', a pub on Byres Road. This was the starting place for the pub crawl, which would eventually lead us to McCormack's Music Shop in Bath Street, where the ultimate accordion was on show, the three-row Hohner, 'Shand Marino'. My friends just wanted to hear me play it, but my objective was to buy it. What with?

One afternoon, while playing to my captivated five-man audience, I noticed a wee man in a bonnet, eyeing me up carefully. Eventually, he made his approach towards his victim: me! 'Would you like one of these accordions?' he asked.

'If I had £200, I'd love one.' I replied.

Cautiously, he slipped his name and address into my pocket. He called himself 'Davy Crockett', with an address on Maryhill Road.

The following day, I bucked up enough courage to visit this guy. One room and one kitchen, known in Glasgow parlance as a 'single end', is what I was admitted to. The room he should have been sleeping in was an Aladdin's cave, with more musical instruments in it than McCormack's shop at 33 Bath Street. The deal was a brand new 'Shand Marino' three-row for £100 (notes of course).

My father and mother sent me down £30, and the remainder was paid out of my student grant money. Chips and lemonade became the staple diet for the rest of that term, coupled with a bag of potatoes and a half barrel of salt herring, from back home. I had almost no money whatsoever, just ha'pennies.

Being a final year physiotherapy student, I had to work during the Christmas holidays. You didn't get any pay for this; it was part of your practical training. It was because of this that on Christmas day 1962, my Christmas dinner consisted of a bottle of lemonade and a fish supper. But to make up for this, on Boxing Day I decided to go hunting for duck in Kelvingrove Park, which was just round the corner from my flat.

I had a pocket full of stones, one of which I let fly at the first duck I saw in the pond. I stunned the duck, dived in after it, rung its neck and put it under my duffle coat. I went away home, plucked it and had it for my dinner.

Musically, this newly acquired 'Rolls Royce' of accordions, set me back quite a bit too, as I had to change my style from 'two-row' to 'three-row' fingering. I persevered until I could easily substitute notes from row one or two onto row three. As the new accordion was obviously 'hot', the standing joke for many years was that if any member of the public turned up at one of our engagements, wearing a hat and raincoat, he was reckoned to be from the CID, coming to arrest me. It was all great fun.

During these student years, my first serious band was formed.

Mike Dowds was a founder member, along with Fiona MacLaren, a student teacher at Jordanhill, and Gordon Fraser, who was studying at the Nautical College. This band was made up of two accordions, piano and drums. Shortly afterwards, we were joined by another pianist, Ian Lawrence; bass player, Noel Eadie; Johnny Hamilton on guitar; and Jimmy Yeaman on fiddle; a wonderful band.

It was during this period that the band was booked for its first big engagement, the 'Wester Ross Gathering'. This was held in the newly-formed 'Highlander's Institute', in Berkley Street, Glasgow. We didn't know it then, but the 'Highlander's', as it was affectionately known, was to become the top meeting place for Gaels in Scotland, with dances full to capacity every Friday and Saturday night throughout the 1960s.

We must have done all right at the Wester Ross Gathering, because, as a result of this, we beat top opposition (thirty bands in all), to land the Saturday night contract at the 'Highlander's' for the next five years. What a kick-start for any aspiring band leader. The band was playing to 500 dancers every Saturday night, with hundreds more locked outside.

The 'Highlander's' was an amazing place in those days. Five hundred was the capacity, and the committee were very strict about this, but there would be as many locked outside again. I used to turn up with maybe as many as twenty band members. Most of them were just friends. One would carry a drumstick, one would have a wee box with PA equipment and so on. They would all get in and then hide until the crowd arrived. The doormen always used to wonder where Fergie's band members had disappeared to.

The police used to be sent along every Saturday to disperse the crowds locked outside on the street. There was never any trouble, as the powers that be always seemed to have the good sense to send Highland policemen. Once the main bulk of the crowd had gone, the policemen would all take off their tunics and come in and join the dance. Can you imagine them getting away with that these days? Before the dance had ended, they would change into uniform and head back to the station.

Saturday night was always party night at the 'Highlander's'. You would finish playing, and all your friends from Acharacle would be waiting for you, dying to know where the party was. Of course, we would have had that organised beforehand. The flats of nurses working in 'the Western' were always favourite venues, and we would be invited along as often as not. I don't think I ever refused one of those parties in my life.

The nurses were always Highland girls, and I have to state now that I have always had the utmost respect for young women from the Highlands. I can assure you that, back then, morals were never abused. It was always great fun, but not like the seedy escapades that one hears of in modern times with dance bands and female company. This was good clean Highland fun. I always respect those girls for that.

The five years I spent at the 'Highlander's' were very, very happy indeed. In many ways, it was the making of me, and helped to put me on the map. The management almost treated me as part of the family. In fact, during my tenure there were two husband and wife teams managing the place: Alasdair MacVicar and his wife, and Archie MacTaggart, from Islay and his good lady.

I had been introduced to this scene by a young man whom I met at the Kilchoan games, a young singer whose mother was from Kilchoan – Cameron MacAulay. Now this guy was just at the top of his form and was due to sing at the games night ceilidh. I went along as a spectator. I always remember him singing a song which was destined to become a big hit, and had just been recorded by Calum Kennedy. 'The Hiking Song' was its name, and Cameron was cheered back onto the stage no less than six times to sing it again. He would come off, the place would erupt, and back he would have to go to sing it once more.

I befriended Cameron and he told me to phone him the minute I arrived in Glasgow. So that is exactly what I did, and he introduced me into all kinds of Highland circles in the city. In fact, Cameron's parents' house was one of the first I visited after arriving in the Glasgow. They were wonderful people.

Cameron showed me the Highland nightlife of swinging Glasgow in the '60s, and believe you me, it was swinging: ceilidhs and dances nearly every night of the week. He used to take me along to all the venues and introduced me to all the influential movers and shakers on the scene. I met all the top band leaders in Glasgow at the time. Big names of that era were Lex Keith and the Cairngorm Dance Band, Iain MacDonald (Cordovox) and the Claymore Dance Band, and brothers Lesley and Andy MacColl.

My studies were a secondary concern at this point, and how on earth I eventually got my degree I shall never know. The good Lord must have been with me. After graduation my first post was as a junior physiotherapist at Lennox Castle Hospital in Lennoxtown. This was pretty demanding work, as it involved the treatment of physically and mentally handicapped patients, both children and adults. In most of the wards the senior nurse had to unlock the door, let in the physiotherapist or doctor, and lock the door behind them. That just shows you what the situation was.

Anyway, on my first morning there, I went to ward five and introduced myself to the senior male nurse. I explained that I was one of the new physios, and he let me into the ward. He invited me to have coffee with the rest of his staff at ten o'clock and I accepted his kind offer, deciding that this would be a good opportunity to meet my new colleagues. 'You've got a Highland accent,' he said.

'So have you,' I replied. That was the start of a wonderful friendship. My new acquaintance was none other than Allan MacKenzie, born and bred in Roshven, Moidart. Allan was a great fiddler and piper, and, as the weeks went by his fiddle and chanter ended up in the staff room of that ward. We would spend half an hour every morning learning tunes. It was Allan who taught me the tune 'Paddy O'Rafferty', with six parts. Funnily enough, I've only ever managed to remember two of them.

I met many wonderful people at this time, many of whom became lifelong friends. Another of these was a young naval cadet officer from Dornie, by the name of Farquhar MacKenzie. Farquhar had been in Glasgow for some time, and was a leading light on the Highland scene, being the captain of the 'Glasgow Inverness-shire' shinty team and a kenspeckle figure at the Highlander's Institute. He was heavily into dancing and ceilidh music and knew all the band leaders well. He said that he would help to get me in on the scene, so as to serve my apprenticeship with one of these bands. He was as good as his word.

Through Farquhar's help I began playing with Lex Keith and the Cairngorm Dance Band. What a wonderful opportunity and what a wonderful experience! I sat in with Lex for a year, listening, watching and learning. I think every young musician who is serious about learning to play for dancing should be encouraged to do something similar. I was very fortunate; I received an excellent grounding. Most of the nights Lex would be joined by other big names, who would sit in for a tune; guys like Bobby MacLeod and Alistair Downie, who had maybe had an engagement earlier in the night.

I have very happy memories of playing in the central belt of Scotland during my stay in Glasgow. New and wonderful experiences seemed to be the order of the day. It was very much a world of its own.

I remember once playing at a dinner dance in Dunblane Hydro, the home venue of the world famous Jim MacLeod Band. It was one of these occasions where each table is named: 'Lord and Lady MacPhail, and party', 'Mr and Mrs John D. MacKenzie, and party'. That was the kind of do that it was. Everyone was dressed in evening wear – the gents in their dinner suits and bow ties, and the ladies in long evening dresses.

The band that I was operating at that time was quite adaptable. We could swing from Scottish music straight into jazz or pop music of the period. The dance went very well, and at the end of the night, after we had played the last waltz, a gentleman who was sitting at the table directly in front of us invited us all to join him for a glass of champagne, which was right up our street. When we had joined him at his table, I remember him snapping his fingers at a waiter, who came bounding over. He ordered two or three bottles of very expensive champagne, which duly arrived on a trolley, encased in buckets of ice. He poured us all a glass, and toasted our health. Very shortly afterwards, one of the waiters came over and told the gentleman that his taxi was waiting for him. It turned out that the taxi was a chauffeur-driven Rolls Royce. Another waiter brought him his white silk scarf and his long black coat, while the rest of his party prepared to leave.

Before he departed he told us to finish off the champagne that was left, and my goodness, we had a ball!

Possibly about a month after this, I happened to be at the famous Barras Market in Glasgow with my first wife, Ann. We were just newly married, and she needed curtains for our kitchen. So on a Sunday afternoon we headed for 'Barrowland' in the east end of the city.

The Barras, like any market or bazaar, can be an amazing place; stall owners and market traders shouting their wears, all offering the best price on the planet. We were looking for a stall selling material or curtains, when I suddenly became aware of this familiar-looking character going through all the usual lines: 'It's not a pound a yard, it's not ten shillings a yard, but eight shillings a yard,' and he would be throwing out rolls of material left, right and centre. Suddenly in the middle of it all, he looked up and shouted: 'Hello Fergie, how are you my friend?' Guess who it was! It was the gentleman from the Dunblane Hydro, who had given us all a glass of champagne and had then been driven home in his Rolls Royce.

That really struck me, but there have been so many amazing incidents. I remember once we were invited to play at Ibrox, the home of the Glasgow Rangers Football Club, at their end-of-season dinner dance, which was to take place on the night of the Scottish Cup Final, when Rangers were due to contest with Celtic. The year was 1969.

The function took place in a palatial suite at the top of the famous 'marble staircase', in the main stand at Ibrox. We had all been looking forward to this night an awful lot. However, tragedy befell us, and it ended up being one of the most miserable dances I ever played at, as Rangers lost the Cup Final to Celtic. What should have been an immensely enjoyable, happy occasion, turned out to be a complete nightmare. I remember all the star players of the time being there. I can vividly remember Willie Henderson, Colin Stein and Ronny MacKinnon, their eyes red-raw with tears. That is how defeat can affect top sportsmen, especially when that defeat comes at the hands of your bitterest rivals.

One of my greatest memories is of that Rangers legend, John Greig, who was then team captain, coming up to sing a song. He was trying to raise morale, and gather the boys together in an attempt to forget the match, but they were obviously intent on drowning their sorrows. The song he sang was the Sinatra classic, 'Strangers in the Night', except that he changed the lyric to 'Rangers in the Night'. It was to no avail. It was one of the most morbid affairs I can remember. We were left wishing that we had been asked to play at a certain victory celebration on the other side of the city.

One of my favourite memories from my days as a young dance band leader is of a dance that we played at not long after the band had been formed. We were just beginning to climb the ladder of dance music success. Young upstarts all, and we probably thought that we knew it all too. There were five of us in the band, and I think we were mostly all students. We were asked to play at a dance in Govan Town Hall, in Glasgow. This represented one of our first major bookings. It was a gathering dance for one of the Highland societies. In those days, if one was asked to play at the Skye Gathering, the Lewis and Harris Gathering, the Tiree Gathering, the Sutherlandshire or any other Gathering, it was a big deal. It was seen as a big step up the ladder; you were just beginning to make it, as they say.

The big night arrived and we were asked to play a couple of selections at the pre-dance concert, which we did, and then the ball started. The ball would run from about eleven o'clock at night until two in the morning. The dance was going very well, until, about one o'clock in the morning, this man appeared at the door dressed in tartan trousers and a tartan dinner-jacket. I always remember that it looked very yellow from where we were sitting. I asked the master of ceremonies, who happened to be Pipe Major Alec MacIvor from Lewis, the composer of the 'Hebridean Polka', who the man wearing all the yellow tartan was. 'That's Bobby MacLeod,' he said.

Well, my Lord. The alarm bells started ringing, right off the reel. He was number one in Scotland at that very moment. We had never met, and there he was as large as life at this gathering. It was the Sutherland Gathering in fact. He had obviously been playing somewhere, probably at the Empire Theatre. When the show was over, he would have headed to this Highland gathering, just to enjoy himself and meet old friends and acquaintances. We were awe-struck. It is amazing how these things affect you.

This was the cue for my band and I to begin playing tunes – jigs and reels that at that time were out of our depth. The yardsticks of dance band musicians in those days were tunes like the 'High Level Hornpipe', 'Mr Wilson's Hornpipe', or 'The Spey in Spate', as a reel. We started belting out such examples mainly to try and impress Bobby MacLeod.

The whole thing began to disintegrate. Our music deteriorated into a rabble, because our fingers suddenly began to freeze. I remember my own fingers were like lumps of lead. In the end, it was an effort to play even Gaelic waltzes, without throwing in some bum notes.

That was our first meeting with Bobby MacLeod. The amazing thing is that the poor man came up to the stage later on and introduced himself to us all. He even asked if we would mind if he sat in with us and had a tune. We were highly honoured! Luckily we were gentlemanly enough to let him go on lead accordion for the wee while that he came up. The poor man, he played tunes which we were so comfortable with: 'The Balmoral Highlanders' and tunes like that. Years and years later, it became a standing joke between Bobby and me, of how we had gone out of our way to impress him. Being the man he was, he understood the situation, joined us on the stage and wished us all the best with our music in the future. From that day forward we became firm friends. There was no longer any need to try and impress the man.

Thinking of this period always puts me in mind of a strange experience I had while playing at a village hall dance in the West Highlands, around that time. If I remember rightly it would have been during the summer; July possibly, around the time of Glasgow Fair. We were still resident at the Highlander's Institute, and had been asked to play at the regatta dance in Kilchoan on a Friday night. We decided to make the return trip to Glasgow after we had finished, so as to keep our engagement in the 'Highlander's' the following night. We reckoned that the dance would finish about three o'clock in the morning, which would mean arriving in Glasgow about half past eight, giving us all a day to catch up on sleep. I travelled to Kilchoan with a three-piece band: bass, drums and Fergie on box. The dance was a rocker, and all was going to plan, as things wrapped up not long after three o'clock.

The end of the night is always traditionally the time for zeroing in on members of the opposite sex, and to this end the drummer approached me and asked for the keys to the car, as he and the other lad had decided to give two young ladies a lift home. I nearly hit the roof. I remember saying, 'For God's sake, do you not remember that we have to leave straight away. I'm giving you fifteen minutes.'

Once the boys had gone, I was left in the hall on my own. The old Kilchoan Hall was a traditional, small, West Highland dance hall, and being a summer's morning the sun was already up. I can remember shafts of sunlight gleaming through the hall windows flanking the dance floor. I was on the stage packing away the equipment when I was suddenly aware of another presence. I looked up to see a young woman standing at the far end of the hall. She was – and I mean this as true as I am standing here – the most beautiful girl I had ever seen in my life. Long blonde hair, wearing a cream blouse and green mini skirt. Not one of these tight ones, but a flared mini skirt that was fashionable at the time. She began to walk towards me. We were both staring at each other, and no more than five metres apart, when I realised that something wasn't right. That instant, she disappeared into thin air.

When the boys returned they could see that I was in an awful, awful state. I told them what had happened. Anyone who knew me at the time would have said that Fergie was pissed, but I wasn't. I knew I had a long journey back to Glasgow ahead of me, and had been careful not to imbibe. I never ever got to the bottom of that mystery, though I have asked countless numbers of people from the Kilchoan area if they knew of any similar occurrences, or any misfortune which may have befallen a young lady with long, flowing blonde hair.

6
The Supernatural

I have been fortunate, or unfortunate, to have had many, many, many supernatural experiences in my lifetime. A lot of the incidents can probably be explained, but many, like my experience in Kilchoan Hall, cannot.

I remember once, while still a physiotherapist, going to the Morar and Mallaig area, which came under my jurisdiction. I left home early on a Wednesday morning and headed for Mallaig, in my red mini metro. It was a beautiful, beautiful morning. I had a list of patients I had to see, in an envelope which lay beside me on the passenger seat. Just as I came towards the railway bridge at Beasdale, between Lochailort and Arisaig, I noticed a hearse, with a coffin in the back, in front of me. There was nothing particularly unusual about this. The hearse would have been about twenty yards ahead of me, and I followed it as it went round the bend before the railway bridge. There is a long straight stretch of road immediately after the railway bridge, maybe two hundred yards or more in length. I took my eye off this hearse and the road ahead, for an instant, while I lifted the list of patients off the passenger seat. I realised that one should not do this while driving, but the road was perfectly straight, and it was for no more than a split second.

When I looked back on the road ahead there was no hearse, nothing at all. It had completely disappeared. There is no way that it could have got out off my sight so quickly, given the very short time period when I had my eye off the road, not to mention the 200 yards of straight highway.

However, I arrived in Mallaig, and the first patient I always had was an old gentleman who was a retired fisherman. His wife came originally from my own neck of the woods – Acharacle. She always had the coffee ready for me, and the conversation was always about her home area: 'What's happening?,' 'Do you see this one, or that one?' etc. On this particular morning I went through my usual routine. I had a heat lamp (an infra-red heat lamp), and I was going in to treat the old fisherman, when his wife met me at the small pathway leading to their house. I had just opened the gate in fact, when she opened the door. I could see that she was upset about something. She spoke to me in Gaelic, saying: 'Fergie a'ghaoil [Fergie darling] you don't have to come in today. Jimmy died at five o'clock this morning.'

This brings us to the interesting point here. The encounter in Kilchoan Village Hall I can find no explanation for; but in this instance I believe I can. My reading of the situation is that the hearse with coffin in it, which I saw only half an hour before, may have been a foretelling of what awaited me on my arrival in Mallaig.

Another example of this, which did not frighten me, happened many years before when I was home on leave from the army. Our next-door neighbour, Bella MacDonald, was very old and was dying. She lived with her son John in a house called 'The Point, Mingarry', which was about a quarter of a mile away from us. It was winter and a very dark night. My mother announced that we were going down to see Bella, to make sure that she didn't want anything, or need anything. That was the way things were in those days. Today, I don't think anyone would bother, supposing you were drawing your last gasps.

We left our cottage, and as we did so, I saw this most amazing white light leaving Bella's house. It lit up the whole of Mingarry. It was a white ball of light, as bright as daylight. It lit up the surrounding countryside. However, the most amazing thing was that my father and mother could not see it. The light left Bella's house and started coming up the road towards us, when suddenly it went out. As we were nearing Bella's house we heard the sound of running, and saw a torch coming towards us. This was Bella's son, John MacDonald. My mother shouted, 'Who's that?' 'It's John,' he replied. 'I can't stop; I'm running up for the priest. My mother has just died.'

Now I am very sure that this bright white light that I saw was connected to this incident. A long time afterwards my father told me that if I had held his hand he would also have seen that light. Whether that is right or wrong I do not know, but that was the understanding that people in Moidart had at that time.

I have also had experiences whereby more than one person has been able to see what I have seen. One that I remember very well involved a man called Alec Wilson, an Edinburgh man. He used to come up to Acharacle with his boss, for the fishing. 'MacTaggart and Scot, of Loanhead', that was the name of the company. They used to have a month's fishing on the Shiel every year, and Alec acted as valet and gillie for his boss. The boss stayed over in Loch Shiel Hotel, and Alec, being the valet, stayed with my mother and father, in digs.

Alec loved fishing, and I was at the age (maybe fifteen or so) where fishing was my big thing. On this particular day (it was a Sunday) we went away up to fish Loch Laga. There is a wee road beside the 'kiosk' at Arivegaig, and if you drive very, very slowly, you can take your vehicle a good way over towards the loch. It's an old peat track, and once you have left your car, you walk a further two miles up the hill to the lochan.

Away we went, and we had a great day that produced a full bag of trout. It was the end of August or early September, getting dark around eight o'clock, and as the twilight descended, we decided to head for home. We came off the hill, and soon hit the road where we had left Alec's car, a green 'Sunbeam Talbot'. We reached the car: Alec went to the driver's side, and I went to the passenger's. We took off our haversacks, and suddenly looked at each other in amazement. The car had completely disappeared in front of our very eyes. It was nowhere to be seen. We could not believe what we had just seen. The car had been there (Alec was just about to open the driver's door), and suddenly it vanished. It reappeared, and I am not exaggerating, about 150 yards round a bend, further on. When we reached the car for a second time, we were able to get in, and drove home without any problems. We have often wondered what exactly happened to that car.

My experiences have never really frightened me. I cannot explain them, but have tried to rationalise them as an extension of my being – another sense if you like. It seems to be genetic, as it exists on both sides of my family. I have no way of knowing whether this will be passed on to my children. Only time will tell.

7

The Right Place at the Right Time

In the early 1960s, when 'Hello Mary-Lou' topped the charts, and the dawn of the 'permissive society' raised the mini skirt hem higher and higher, I got my opportunity to enter the world of theatre. Although I was performing regularly at ceilidhs and dances, I most certainly was not equipped to prance onto a stage and perform solo, grinning from ear to ear. This is generally known in the business as stage presentation.

This new twist in my musical career began in the most bizarre of fashions. There was a twelve-week summer show in progress at the Metropole Theatre, Stockwell Street, Glasgow. Will Starr was the accordionist, included in a cast of comics, dancers, singers, magicians, etc. Will Starr was nothing short of being a genius on the accordion, but he suffered from a terrible alcohol addiction, causing the poor man to drop out of the show.

Wednesday's evening paper carried an advert which read: 'Accordionist wanted at the Metropole Theatre. Auditions at eleven o'clock tomorrow morning, at the theatre.' The 'box' and I caught the 44 bus to Jamaica Bridge, got off, and walked to the theatre in Stockwell Street.

After waiting for about half an hour in the front row of an empty theatre, I suddenly realised that no other accordionist had turned up. Eventually, the adjudicating panel of producer, director and musical director appeared and sat themselves down where I was sitting. They jotted down my name, and promptly ordered me to perform in front of them, on the massive empty stage. As no other accordionist had appeared, it was taken as read that I had the job, as the director required somebody to perform that very evening, in full Highland dress. First stop was Henderson's Highland Outfitters, on Renfield Street. I had never worn full Highland dress before. The manager of the shop even managed to talk me into wearing a long hairy sporran, which was down to my knees – the type the Highland regiments wore into battle.

On arrival at the theatre in the early evening, the musical director, Mr Masterton, asked me for the scores. Now, I thought he was talking about the football pools, as Rangers and Celtic were playing a cup-tie that evening. The musical interpretation of 'score' means sheet music, and band parts for the pit orchestra. This was impossible, as I couldn't read or write music. Time was not on our side. It was too late for Mr Masterton to write the parts out himself, so I hummed and diddled my proposed selections to him. Can you imagine? He was not amused.

'We'll try and busk it,' he said, 'and sort out this mess tomorrow morning.'

My turn soon came to stand in the wings and wait for my cue to run onto the stage and start playing my tunes. The producer told me to stand at the spot on the stage marked with an X, and wait for my microphone to appear. I obviously ran out too quickly, and misjudged the spot marked X. I could find no microphone. Little did I know that I was standing directly over the spot where the electrically controlled microphone would pop up through a tiny hole in the stage floor, reaching the required height of about four feet, in order for me to be heard playing the accordion. Having no theatre experience whatsoever, and deprived of the benefit of a rehearsal, I thought someone was going to run out on stage and place a microphone in front of me, as used to happen at the ceilidhs I was so used to playing at. I was suddenly aware of a cold microphone head going upwards under my kilt, and lodging itself in my private parts. It pushed my hairy sporran straight out in front of me at a ninety-degree angle. In actual fact, the situation was really frightening, as I did not know what the hell was going on, or what was really happening. The audience were rolling with laughter. They were in hysterics. Instead of jigs and reels coming through the speakers, and filling the theatre with music, they were treated to a noise more akin to thunder, as the sensitive microphone scraped against my bollocks, throwing out the most amazing noises and sounds. The resident comedian, Billy Rusk, was not amused in the slightest, I obviously drew more laughs from the audience than he did that night.

Anyway, on the strength of my performance, the producer offered me a contract for the remaining nine weeks of the show. This was a new world to a lad brought up in the wilds of Moidart and Ardnamurchan. Parties seemed to be the order of the day, and my first brush with homosexuality was about to take place. The world of show business seemed so unreal to me. Everybody would address each other as 'darling', and kiss each other, irrespective of gender, at every conceivable opportunity.

My moment of reckoning came at a party thrown by members of the ballet, who were appearing along the road, at the Alhambra Theatre. The party was held in a huge big flat on Great Western Road. By the time I arrived, at one o'clock in the morning, the party was in full swing. I remember being most cordially welcomed by the host, who was the guy in charge of the ballet dancers. Everything was spot on; plenty of delicate eats, and booze everywhere, low lights, throbbing music, and most of the guests dressed in such a way as to leave little to the imagination. Just the perfect set-up for a young buck like myself, until disaster struck.

I was sitting on a beautiful, wine-coloured sofa, with a large gin and tonic, when the host sat himself down beside me. This guy was the male lead dancer, and his body was identical to pictures one sees of 'Mr Universe'. Men would give the world to have such a masculine physique. Like the perfect host he got me another gin, and sat down next to me again. He slipped his arm round my shoulder. This was no big deal – just a friendly guy, I thought.

By this time, the lights were really low, and couples were groping each other on the dance floor, when out of the blue, with no warning whatsoever, this guy slipped his hand right up my kilt. Instinctively, I leapt to my feet, in a state of utter shock, and gave him a verbal volley: 'You dirty bastard!' I shouted. I had no mates with me otherwise I would have stretched him there and then. The situation was risky. I grabbed my jacket, walked out, and flagged down the first taxi that came my way, going straight home to my flat.

Incidentally, I only ever met the man whom I replaced in that summer show once. It was on a Sunday afternoon in the Cameron Highlander's Club in Inverness, sometime during the '60s. I had just popped in for a drink. Who was sitting there in the corner but Will Starr. He had a table full of drams, the like of which I had never seen before. I went over and introduced myself and explained that I could knock a tune out of the box. I was stunned when he offered me a shot of his own accordion. He was very impressed with me and said: 'Fergie son, I'll have to show you a wee thing.' He showed me how to execute a 'birl', which is a form of triplet, on the button box. I have used the same technique ever since.

I rated Will Starr so highly. He was undoubtedly a genius. The funny thing was, his background in music was very different to that of your average button-key accordionist. Most of us were just self-taught, but Will Starr had received some formal tuition. He had been given lessons by an Italian who owned an ice-cream parlour in the Milton of Campsie area. Will Starr, who was a miner from Croy, got to know this chap. The Italian gentleman was apparently a very gifted accordionist, and of course he played in a very continental style. This would probably account for Starr's own fondness for continental music. His Italian tutor taught him everything he needed to know about fingering and button-box technique. It certainly stood him in good stead and placed him ahead of the game. He was a strange combination of extremes in many ways. He was a technical genius and could do things with the accordion that ordinary mortals could not even dream of. Yet he found it difficult to play the easiest of tunes straight. He just couldn't do it. He had to load everything with trills, tricks and embellishments. In a way, he was probably like me. He would never have made it in a Scottish country dance band. He would never have had the temperament or the discipline. He was far too creative for all that. We will never see his like again. He had the most brilliant fingers that I ever heard and will probably ever hear. He was a true master of his art.

This period in the world of theatre taught me the very important art of stage presentation. It was drilled into me that the most basic factor was the ability to smile during a performance. During the last week of the summer show, indeed at the final performance, a gentleman called John M. Bannerman was among the invited guests. I didn't know it, but John M. Bannerman was just about to change my life forever.

8
Television

Lord John M. Bannerman is the gentleman responsible for introducing me to the world of television. At the end of the last show in the Metropole, John Bannerman, who was an invited guest, made his way to my dressing room. After he had introduced himself he told me of a television programme that he was to present for Scottish Television. The programme, entitled 'Highland Air', required a Gaelic-speaking team, comprising two singers, an instrumentalist, a presenter and a well-known personality, who was to be taught a couple of well-known Gaelic phrases on each episode. I was asked to be the instrumentalist.

The cast did its first transmission on Scottish Television in the spring of 1964. Lord Bannerman was the 'anchor man', or, in the language of Gaeldom, *Fear an Taighe*. The supporting cast included the writer and broadcaster, Jack House; Evelyn Campbell and Alasdair Gillies, both young mod gold medallists; and finally Fergie, the young West Highland accordionist.

The first series amounted to fourteen weekly half-hour shows of Gaelic music and song. Almost immediately after its very first showing, 'Highland Air' slotted into the charts of the top-ten Scottish television programmes. It got off to a flier. One of the highlights in relation to the series, was the rehearsals. Every weekend John Bannerman would hold rehearsals at his farm, near Balmaha, on the shores of Loch Lomond. The rehearsals usually ended up as full-blown ceilidhs. The house would be jam packed with prospective guest artistes, family and friends. Lady Bannerman would feed us with the most wonderful traditional Highland dishes, always starting with her own special

Scotch broth. She used to keep my special delicacy on a plate, through in the kitchen. She knew that the lamb shank, with which she made the broth, was what I liked best. Discreetly, in the kitchen, I would be holding both ends of the shank, and eating straight off the bone. Lord and Lady Bannerman simply adored this uncouth Highland approach to eating. By the way, until recently, John Bannerman held the record for being the most capped Scottish rugby player at international level. It is amazing that his record stood for so long, given the fact that players, nowadays, receive caps for friendly matches and such like.

'Highland Air' became a very popular programme, extending to a three-year run of weekly shows. Invitations to appear in subsequent television programmes soon followed. Inevitably, the stamp of 'TV personality' gave my music another dimension. Over the years I must have made hundreds of television appearances; seldom ever do I watch any programme that I perform in. It's like looking through a window at a scene you happen to be part of, but feel that it's not really you. It's almost like watching a totally different human being from what you imagine yourself to be. You become your own worst critic, not so much musically, but of the way that you portray yourself. The worst part can be the highlighting of what you feel are physical deficiencies. I have often felt so silly when someone enquires as to whether you 'enjoyed the programme the other night' or not. Having spoken to other television personalities, I have found that the phenomenon of not watching oneself is a fairly common one.

The first producer I ever worked with was David Bell, who started with Scottish Television and went on to greater things with London Weekend Television. He had an uncanny knack of getting the best out of artistes and helping them to relax in front of the cameras. In those days there were very few places one could go to learn about those kinds of things. David was very generous with his time, and would always be willing to help and encourage. I learnt so much about studio technique from him; how to perform on camera, how to know when the camera was on you, and wee things like that. The bottom line for him was that you always had to look happy: 'Smile,' he would say 'it's not a funeral.' He was, in my opinion, a genius, and well ahead of his time. Unfortunately, he had been head-hunted, and moved to London before the end of the series. I often used to see his name as producer of the Royal Variety Performance and shows like that. His passing, at an early age, was a tragedy. I reckon that television lost one of its greats.

One day, while filming 'Highland Air', David Bell couldn't get the cast and film crew to stop laughing. They were filming Alasdair Gillies singing the 'Loch Tay Boat Song', while he rowed a boat, with Fergie sitting in the stern, playing the box. Suddenly, our kilts were round our ears, as the boat keeled over on its side in the studio. We were sprawling about on the studio floor, still singing and playing the box. These calamities happen all the time during the making of programmes, and I have often felt that most of these tragic mistakes should be shown, as some are really hilarious.

Another time, while recording a programme called 'Fireside Ceilidh', a chunk of my accordion, called the 'grill', simply fell off. Why don't these things happen while playing the box in the kitchen?

I am lucky enough to have been involved in many other television productions since those halcyon days. Many things have changed, but the overall professionalism and dedication to producing material of the highest quality within the television industry have not.

One of my favourite producers at the moment is John Smith from the BBC. John has been at the helm of many productions, most notably the BBC 'Hogmanay Live' shows, which have been a huge success. John is another producer who knows how to put you at your ease. In my case I think he had to, because during one of these shows the first notes of the New Year were to be played by Fergie and his band. What an honour! Luckily, to hold my hand musically, I had Phil Cunningham sitting beside me.

Another favourite of mine has always been John Carmichael, from Islay. We have worked together on numerous productions for Gaelic television over the years. John is incredibly down-to-earth and understands the needs of the Highland band leader.

There are also some new directors and producers on the scene these days. It is encouraging to see that they are willing to show a bit of imagination in their work. They like to try things. One of the leading lights of this new school is Bob Kenyon, based at Grampian Television in Aberdeen. Bob is always keen to give new and emerging talent a chance to shine, and always seems to find space in his youthful line-ups for yours truly. I like that!

Another of the new wave is Duncan MacDonald from the Isle of Skye. Duncan has all the ingredients to be a superb director and producer. He is extremely creative, imaginative and able to improvise when things go slightly off kilter. After all, you just never know what will happen next, especially in live television.

I remember once, performing on a Gaelic production called *De a Nis?*, which was presented by Cathy MacDonald. My hands were very sweaty, so I produced my little tin of Johnson's Baby Powder and applied it to my hands. Just as I was putting it on, we suddenly went on air. There I was with this tin of baby powder, which I had to ditch and begin playing. The BBC received hundreds of letters in the following weeks enquiring as to whether all the top musicians were using baby powder!

9

The First Album

By 1963 the personnel of the band had changed. The line-up was now: Fergie, on button-box; Gordon Fraser on piano-box; Mike Dowds on drums; Ian Lawrence on piano and Johnny Cochrane on double bass.

Politically, musicians were brainwashed into believing that Scottish country dance music was the only way forward. Ceilidh music was severely frowned upon. It was for this reason that musicians from the Highlands and Islands were looked upon as second and third rate. They were classed in the same bracket as traditional Irish ceilidh bands. The powers that be were really more interested, accordion-wise, in what chords one was churning out with one's left hand. Great emphasis was placed on piano and double bass chords and arrangements, coupled with another accordion, belting out more chords. The lead instruments, accordion and fiddle, had to play in complete unison, exactly note for note.

This kind of music was aimed at the hundreds of new country dances, which had been devised by various individuals. Scotland was sold on this kind of music for three-quarters of the twentieth century. If you didn't comply you didn't play, simple as that. Scottish music was based on this ridiculous format.

As a means to an end, I also had to conform. In those days, if you wished to enter the record business, you had to apply for an audition. Today, any third-rate musician (or band) can approach any one of several hundred recording companies, and they will record you and release a CD. The result is that nowadays we have a market flooded with third-rate artistes, and third-rate recordings. There's controversy at its best for you! The artistes, or bands, suddenly become recording stars, selling their products in the local village store, craft shop or petrol station. It's a catch twenty-two situation. The recording company want money, the recording artistes want to become stars, and there are no rules or guidelines on how each achieves their aims.

Being ambitious, I approached Waverley Records, the Scottish branch of EMI in Edinburgh. After hearing our demonstration tape, they invited us for an audition. The selection board, somehow, gave us pass-marks, and the band was signed up for a five-year contract. We were given one day to record and complete the album, comprising twelve tracks. Amazingly, we managed to record eleven tracks, but after fifteen attempts at the Eightsome Reel, we were asked to come back the following Saturday to finish off.

The week passed very quickly, and I remember playing at a dance in Govan Town Hall on the Friday night. We all attended a party following the dance and we were still so drunk in the morning that none of us could drive. We took the train through to Edinburgh, got a taxi and piled into the studio. The producer, Bryce Laing (whom I knew for years afterwards), and the sound engineer, gave us a quick run through. Bryce Laing asked us if we were ready for a take. It was a unanimous 'yes' from the band. There were ten different tunes in this particular Eightsome Reel track, and I distinctly remember playing the last tune, which was 'Mrs MacLeod of Raasay'. At that point I knew we were 'all clean', as we say in the business. That meant there had been no 'balls-ups' so far. It is the only time in my life I can remember combining a tune with a prayer. I remember saying to myself, 'please God let us go straight'. We did. After getting the tunes in the can, we really went on the piss in Edinburgh, to celebrate our new-found success. We reckoned that we were big-time recording stars.

The recording techniques in those days were very basic, as you would expect. One microphone was the norm, and would be placed in the middle of the room. That was that. It was a case of trying to achieve the proper sound balance by moving the various musicians and instruments around the studio. Proximity to the microphone was the key. The poor drummer would often find himself out in the hallway. He would have to be cued in by relay.

Studio engineers and producers were doing their level best with next to nothing in those days. Their equipment and techniques were very crude. That was not their fault. It was just the way of things. I suppose that many of these guys were just enthusiasts, learning their trade as they went. Nowadays you're dealing with top producers like Phil Cunningham and Addie Harper, who know their work inside-out and have access to the most up-to-date technology at their finger tips.

Waverley, in all honesty, were fairly advanced compared to most record labels at that time. They had a state-of-the-art studio in Edinburgh, with a properly equipped control room, staffed by recording engineers and technicians. Some of the band were even allowed their own microphone. The drummer was always a problem though. In fact, it's funny, but even though recording techniques have developed beyond belief, the drummer is still often a problem in this day and age.

When the long-playing record (LP) was released, I, for one, was disappointed with the cover. It was really drab, with nothing exciting about it whatsoever. By the end of the first financial year of our contract, the album had sold 400 copies. The royalties amounted to £4 10s. The cheque was accompanied by a tactfully written letter, advising us that our album had been a disaster, and that our five-year contract had been terminated forthwith. This was the first big disappointment of many which were to follow.

A fascinating sequel to this sorry tale was that Shona Records bought the master tape from EMI ten years later, changed the name of the album from 'Dance to Your Partner' to 'It's Scotland's Music' – a play on the topical SNP campaign of the time, entitled 'It's Scotland's Oil' – and sold 10,000 copies in the first year alone.

That, however, was for the future. We were in the recording wilderness, following our recording début fiasco.

10
Broadcasting

Being termed a 'broadcasting band' was always the ultimate accolade for any Scottish dance band. Strangely enough, it is still the yardstick by which all bands are judged, even now in the twenty-first century. I advise any band leader to have a go at the BBC audition for Scottish dance music. The result will soon tell you whether you have what it takes to succeed, or whether you are living in a world of fantasy.

During the 1960s, broadcasting bands enjoyed the stature of pop stars. The giants in this field were Jimmy Shand, Bobby MacLeod, Jim MacLeod, The Wick Scottish Dance Band, Ian Powrie, The Hawthorn Scottish Dance Band, Alasdair Downie, Jim Cameron, Alan Williams, Hamish Menzies and Max Houlston, to name but a few.

To break into that field was almost an impossible task. Anyhow, we applied for the audition, and passed it with flying colours first time, in April 1965. It was a typical Scottish country dance band set-up. I was on lead accordion, Jimmy Yeaman was on fiddle, Mike Dowds was on drums, Calum Kenmuir on piano and Noel Eadie on bass.

Our first broadcast was recorded at the BBC's Edinburgh studios in June 1965. Transmission was in early July. On that particular Saturday night the band was playing at Bridge of Orchy. We tuned into the BBC home service at seven o'clock and heard ourselves for the first time, sitting in a car outside Bridge of Orchy Hotel. We were more nervous listening to it than we had been recording it. It was a tremendous honour to join this elite group of top Scottish bands, but it didn't give me, personally, the lift that it should have. To be very honest, it was just like listening to any one of a hundred other broadcasting bands.

The BBC producer was James Hunter, a musical genius, but pickled in the BBC's strict version of how Scottish country dance music should be played. Personally, I found the whole thing extremely boring. It was a million miles away from the *craic* ceilidh music that I was brought up with in the Highlands.

After a few programmes, my personal revolution began. This was probably the start of the entire revolution, which changed the face of Scottish music many years later. The sedate 'Strathspey' country dance tunes were substituted for mouth music 'Strathspeys', which were more suited to a Highland schottische or Scotch Reel in Ness Village Hall, for example. Ceilidh-type jigs and reels were slotted into place, as opposed to the strict tempo tunes suitable for dances like Scottish Reform and Hamilton House. My idea was to play up-tempo ceilidh music for these country dances. What a rebel!

The plan went into operation during a recorded dance music programme from Dundee. I remember Ian Holmes was finishing his programme as we arrived. He wished us good luck. If only he had known.

The boys and I put in a flawless performance. Everything went 'in the can' first take, with no repeats. Sound engineers, floor managers, secretaries and even the wee woman making our tea, thought our programme was outstanding. Unfortunately, they were the only ones that thought so. Shortly afterwards, a letter arrived from the BBC with no accompanying cheque. I thought this very strange. It read:

'Dear Mr MacDonald, your broadcasting contract with the BBC has been terminated, as of now. Your choice of music was not in keeping with the type of music that we associate with our Scottish dance music programmes. Your fiddle player was totally out of order, and had great difficulty in playing some of the notes. You are therefore suspended from future broadcasts, until such time as you re-sit your audition.' That's *craic* isn't it?

I loved the reference to the fiddle player. Poor Jimmy Yeaman was under strict orders from me to slur and slide all kinds of notes, in order to give the music more lift and swing. His fiddle-playing became almost 'Country' or 'Bluegrass' in style.

So that was us out on our ears again, and it was to be an awful long time before an amazing change in events occurred. Thirty years later I received a letter from the BBC inviting me back as a broadcasting band, and giving me a warrant to play even more outrageous ceilidh-type music. This was what I had been expelled for, thirty years before. By the time I was invited back, I had established ceilidh music in its truest form, as an accepted genre of dance music in Scotland. The modern team of Robbie Shepherd and Ken Mutch at the BBC got the message. They understood just how popular this kind of music was, and invited me back.

Things have changed so much though. When I started broadcasting, it was basically all down to the band whether that particular broadcast was a success or not. Nowadays, it's a very different story. We were never allowed a second go at recording things (that's if we were allowed the luxury of a recording session at all, as most broadcasts were live). These days you can re-record, edit, splice and overdub things until the artiste is happy. In short, you are given the opportunity to doctor the whole thing up. That basically means that anyone can achieve a good sound. Musicians become musically infallible. Is that a good thing? I'm not sure. I'm really not a believer in this at all. I'm of the old school. I believe that you should be judged on your performance. Even yet, I insist (usually) on using the first take. My last broadcast had sixteen items on it and only one re-take (due to a technical fault). I'm not saying that they were absolutely note perfect, but that's the Fergie sound and that's the way I do it; natural, good, wholesome music. If there is a little blip, then I can live with that, as long as it is not a complete calamity. That is the way it should be. There are so many bands now, churning out flawless broadcasts, whom you wouldn't cross the street to hear live. They are just not able to reproduce the heavily manufactured sound of their broadcasts. They are not doing themselves any favours. I reckon that hearing natural talent raw is what broadcasting is all about.

Some things have definitely changed for the better. Directors and producer are, these days, so much more adept at putting the artiste at ease. In my younger days a broadcast could end up being an absolute pressure-cooker of a situation. It is an awful lot more enjoyable nowadays. In fact, it has become quite a sociable event.

This is in no small part due to the efforts and professionalism of the aforementioned Robbie Shepherd and his producer, Ken Mutch. It is an extremely nerve-racking experience for any young musician, but these guys have got 'putting the artiste at ease' down to a fine art – to work with them is a pleasure.

11
Composing

I drifted into the world of composition by complete accident. My first attempt was really just for a laugh. As I describe more fully later in the book, the inspiration arose from a visit to an illegal drinking den on the island of Lewis, known as a 'bothan'. I wrote a jig which I called 'Ness Bothan'. Amazingly, it lay dormant for many, many years until I recorded it, which brought little reaction or success. The tune was eventually recorded by the Wick Scottish Dance Band, and then the flood-gates opened. Robert MacLeod from Tobermory, and many more, took it on. I suppose that that really led on to lots of other compositions: 'Maureen's Jig', 'The Dark Waters of Loch Shiel' and 'The Jig Runrig', to name but a few. I must have, by now, at least 100 compositions to my name.

What I find is, that with all these compositions, you have to have an element of luck. You have to be in the right place at the right time, as they say. Not that I am taking away from the fact that the tune, or melody, must have something about it that somebody likes. It is very difficult, though, to hit on a winner. I know so many brilliant musicians and composers who have made many tunes, but none of them have ever become musical standards, or everyday tunes that musicians would play. I consider myself very fortunate.

One of the compositions that really took off was 'The Jig Runrig'. So far, it has been recorded by over fifty bands, groups and artistes all over the world. There is even a fiddler from Canada, a Cherokee Indian, who has recorded it. The tune was originally to be called 'Memories of Baille Cnocan'. But on meeting Phil Cunningham in Inverness one day, and sharing a vindaloo with him, he recommended that the name should be changed. I sang the tune over to him, and he thought it was brilliant. He asked me what the name was and I told him the intended title. By the way, 'Baille Cnocan' is a sexual encounter at a ceilidh. Phil's reckoning was that Robbie Shepherd, the presenter of BBC Radio Scotland's Scottish dance music programme would have great difficulty in pronouncing it.

I went home and sat on it for a while, before phoning Phil and asking him what he thought of 'The Jig Runrig'. He thought it was a wonderful idea, although I insisted that the boys from Runrig hear the tune first. As luck would have it, Phil was appearing somewhere with them, and he played it over to them. They were delighted and bought the idea right off the reel. That has really become a very, very famous tune, and most Scottish musicians play it.

There are lots and lots of others: 'The Shinty Referee', made for Henry MacInnes from Portnalong, 'Donnie MacGillivray', for a local bus and transport magnate. Donnie wanted a tune made for him, and ended up waiting twenty years for it. I also made a tune for Bishop Roddy Wright, whom I admire so much. He is a man's man. He made up his own mind, and did what he thought was right. Then, to balance things up, I composed one for Donald Findlay, the very famous QC. He was caught on video singing 'The Sash'. I personally couldn't see anything at all wrong with that, but the poor man was hounded for his choice of music. I decided that he definitely deserved a tune written for him. Both men are over the moon with their respective compositions. In fact, they both received first copies of the albums that their tunes were recorded on.

Composing has taken me a long way in the world of music. I have coupled that with the recent formation of my own recording and publishing company, 'Rannoch Recordings'. So far we have two albums to our credit, 'Ceilidh House' and 'Jiggy Jig'.

The name of the second album has caused much hilarity, humour and controversy in Highland circles. It is, of course, a term used very loosely by Highland soldiers and sailors while on manoeuvres in the Orient and the Middle East. I would always hear guys talking about 'Jiggy Jig', which always intrigued me. Finding out what it was intrigued me even more. I thought that 'Jiggy Jig' was a wonderful name, as it carries a suggestion of our own jigs, which we play. Couple that with the other meaning of 'Jiggy Jig', and you have the recipe for a wonderful night out.

Having my own recording and publishing company has given me complete control over my music, but this was not always the case. It was only really as a result of bitter experience that I decided to act in the first place. The world of composition is full of pitfalls. Everyone wants to make a buck out of your talents. Young musicians are especially vulnerable, and I would like to give them a word of warning. This insight is gained from mistakes I made myself during my younger days.

When you realise that you have created a tune, you are so overwhelmed and happy that, as a young musician, you tend to forget about copyrights, publishing rights and legal rights of all sorts.

As I mentioned earlier, one of my first compositions was a tune called 'Ness Bothan'. It was pretty insignificant at the time, but a good tune nevertheless. I myself recorded it in the early 1970s on the Grampian record label. When the record company were taking down the tune titles, composers and publishers, the producer asked me if 'Ness Bothan' was one of my own. I told him it was, and he wanted to know about the tune's copyright details. I explained that I didn't know anything about that.

'I'll just leave all that up to you,' I said.

'That's fine,' he said, 'just leave it to us and we'll sort it.'

I did as he said and left them to it. I was just happy that I was getting the tune recorded.

A few years after that, Addie Harper of the Wick Scottish Dance Band heard 'Ness Bothan' and phoned me with a request to record it. He also wanted to know what the situation was regarding copyright. 'Nothing,' I said, 'I've only recorded it myself.' 'Well,' he replied, 'I have my own music publishing company, and we'll do all the copyrighting and publishing for you, if you want.' He told me that this would make sure that I held all the rights to the tune, which I believed, as Addie Harper was one of the very few honest people in the music industry. So that, as far as I was concerned, was everything taken care of. Addie's album, with 'Ness Bothan' on it, did very well and everything was rosy.

The BBC then contacted me to see if they could use 'Ness Bothan' as a signature tune on one of their Gaelic radio programmes, Morag MacDonald's *Mire ri Mor.* I was delighted to say yes to their request. This meant that almost overnight 'Ness Bothan' took off. It was played daily for years as a signature tune, and bands everywhere were picking it up and recording it. Suddenly, this insignificant little tune had become viable in financial terms. Addie's publishing company were receiving the six-monthly cheques from the Performing Rights Society in London, and being the gentleman that he was, he would send me my dues right away. It was the perfect arrangement.

Then all of a sudden a letter arrived one day from the legal department of a company called Campbell & Connolly, who were another publishing group of whom I had never heard. On reading the letter, however, I was left in no doubt as to what they wanted from me. It seemed that they now held the original copyright for 'Ness Bothan' from the recording I had made for Grampian Records. They demanded massive sums of money, which they believed they were due on back-dated royalties. I was suddenly diverted from a joyful, happy world of making music, to the harsh realities of the financial minefield that is the world of publishing and copyright. It took years to sort out this terrible mess, all because of a young inexperienced musician (namely myself), who knew nothing about the business side of things, and was happy enough to go along with the flow, pretending that everything was all right.

My advice to all aspiring musicians is that, if you compose a tune, whether it is good, bad or indifferent, get it copyrighted straight away, so that nobody can cut in and demand any form of payment from you. You may not think anything of your composition, but who knows what's around the corner? It could easily be taken onboard by a major musical institution or company like the BBC. You just never know; but at least if it is copyrighted you are ready for all eventualities.

12
Political Comment

To succeed as a band leader in the field of Scottish dance music, you have to prove that you are able to mould a broadcasting band successfully.

As you now know, in order to broadcast on the BBC dance music programmes, one has to pass a very trying audition. The basic ingredient required is a note-perfect performance. If any of the musicians in your band cannot produce thirty minutes of flawless music, then you have failed. It's as simple as that. To take it a stage further, dance bands which do pass are technically perfect – the best that Scotland has to offer. On the down side, my opinion is that with such perfection Scottish dance bands have become generally boring. The most disturbing factor is the lack of imagination pertaining to sound, and the extreme lack of 'kick' or 'lift' in the music. This lifeless motionless music seems to lend itself perfectly to Scottish country dances and classes.

North of Crianlarich, forget it! That is why, nowadays, a broadcasting band means very little on the Highland circuit. The ball-game has changed dramatically. Ceilidh bands are now the 'in' thing. In all honesty, they were never away – just not recognised. Ceilidh bands were seen as the poor relations of the Scottish dance world, right up until the 1980s, when I myself broke away from mainstream Scottish dance music and put Ceilidh music on the map.

Just before the Second World War, Sir Jimmy Shand had begun to produce a sound which before the end of the 1940s became world famous. Jimmy opened the door for us all, in relation to Scottish dance music. A hard-working miner from Fife, Jimmy's music was based on village hall dances, at which he served his apprenticeship. Jimmy Shand set the format of button accordion, fiddle, piano, bass and drums. The standard sound – recognised the world over – of Scottish dance music.

Other band leaders followed; Andrew Rankine, Ian Powrie, Jimmy Blair, Dougal Jenkins, Jim Cameron, Alasdair Downie and Adam Rennie, to name but a few. Every one of those band leaders, and their bands, had a very distinctive sound. All were broadcasting bands of great quality, but with individual style, and above all with 'lift' in the music.

Everybody talked about an east-coast/west-coast divide. They reckoned that east-coast bands didn't have the west-coast sound, and weren't as good. This is utter rubbish. Every band I have mentioned had their own unique sound and lift, developed through playing at barn dances, bothy dances and village hall dances. I doubt if any of these great names ever came through the system of lessons, teachers or '*feis* classes'. They were naturally talented musicians.

I would like to add to the above list of luminaries, two of the greatest bands of all time: Bobby MacLeod and his Highland Band, from Tobermory, and Addie Harper's Wick Scottish Dance Band.

Bobby Macleod's first instrument was the bagpipes. This gave him an excellent grounding in pipe music. It was probably second nature for him to incorporate pipe tunes into an accordion repertoire. Through the mediums of broadcasting and recording, Bobby made the playing of pipe music popular with Scottish dance bands the world over. We thank Bobby MacLeod for his contribution. Needless to say, he was the master of this art.

When I think of the Wick Scottish Dance Band, variety is the keyword. In the course of an evening they could produce at least ten different sounds. The bottom line was, however, that you could dance to this band. Addie Harper's band travelled from Wick to every corner of Scotland every weekend of the year. They were the most popular 'circuit' band going, for decades.

For sheer brilliance on the accordion, the name of Alan Williams from Inverness must be at the forefront. I remember Alan playing a set of tunes on a live Scottish dance music programme once. The set of tunes (and this was live) included such technically demanding pieces as 'Mr Wilson's Hornpipe', 'The Spey in Spate', and the 'High Level Hornpipe'. It was absolutely flawless playing. How about that?

I think what did more harm to Scottish dance music than anything else was the introduction of what is known in the business as the 'second box'. Probably, whoever introduced a second accordion as a means of accompanying a lead accordion, had good intentions, but the idea progressed to the stage where all bands introduced this distinctive sound. The music became monotonous, predictable, and as dead as a door nail. Most of the time the second box played chords, completely lacking in imagination. The only band that kept any sort of individuality while using two accordions was the Wallochmor Dance Band. Sandy Coghill and Freeland Barbour produced an exciting sound by playing in unison, but in different registers.

Towards the end of the 1990s I was delighted to see that many Scottish dance bands were once again using just five instruments: accordion, fiddle, drums, piano and bass. The second box was starting to disappear. Slowly but surely, bands were starting to develop their own sounds again, which can only be achieved, really, by highlighting the lead instruments. As a very famous producer from the BBC, namely Fred MacAuley, once said: 'Who the hell, in Lochmaddy, will be listening to Fergie's left hand?'

This statement was made during a debate concerning which accordionist would get a 'spot' on a particular Gaelic television broadcast. Basically, it means that the general public listen to the melody, but are only aware of the overall sound. Without bass, piano or guitar, the overall sound would be spineless, but a band lives or dies by the lead instruments.

13
Overseas

Nowadays, Scottish musicians and groups seem to spend a lot of their time overseas. This creates one or two difficulties as far as I am concerned. Part of the problem stems from the fact that musicians, maybe after one or two album releases, or radio or television shows, believe themselves to be superstars. A trip to Singapore, to play at a 'Burns night', for example, will be highlighted by the media, causing more problems. When people read about these trips, human reasoning assumes that these musicians are on another planet, and are above playing venues like 'Ballachulish Village Hall'. Eventually, these 'superstars' lose the plot completely, and in a comparatively short period of time are just names of the past. How many big names are around for a few years, and then disappear?

When I started out with the band, making our début on the continent was a big deal. We thought we were big news too, you see. We were invited to play at a St Andrew's Night Ball in Copenhagen. Luckily, I was able to bring my full broadcasting band with me, minus Jimmy Yeaman, our regular fiddle-player. In his place came Farquhar MacRae, from Lochailort. My band was joined on this trip by Pipe Major Angus MacDonald (North Uist), of the City of Glasgow Police Pipe Band, and his colleague Murdo MacDonald, from the island of Lewis.

On jetting into Copenhagen from Glasgow, I remember distinctly the climatic shock we all experienced. Having left mild, wet Glasgow, we were met by snow and ice, and a temperature about five degrees below freezing. We all stayed at the Hotel Angleterre, getting VIP treatment of course.

Having dined at the banquet, with members of the Danish Royal Family, it was time to get the ball rolling, so to speak. The programme consisted of twenty Scottish country dances, many of which were fairly standard, like the 'Duke of Perth', 'Reel of the 51st' and 'Hamilton House'. It was the first time that any of the band had come into contact with exiles, or ex-pats, and that certainly hit a raw nerve. You suddenly realised that you were not only a musician, but an ambassador for Scotland. You are suddenly in the shop window, helping to portray the good image of Scots in general. Meeting tears from Scots abroad drums home to you just what a strong patriotic feeling these people have for their homeland; more so when the conversation is in Gaelic. Having witnessed all this, it was only a matter of time before Gaelic culture reared its beautiful head. It came in the shape of Donny MacDonald from Ness in Lewis, who leapt onto the stage and belted out *Balaich an Iasgaich*.

By the end of the ball, we had our own wee ceilidh in a corner of the ballroom; singing Gaelic songs and belting out tunes on the box, for a Highland schottische. Wherever Gaels meet, they always return to their own culture. I think sometimes that that is when Lowland Scots wish they were blessed with our Gaelic heritage. They suss out that they are missing out on something very important.

In the early hours of the morning, Donny took us on a tour of Copenhagen's nightspots. Schnapps and Carlsberg Special were the order of the day, to such an extent that I fell asleep during a live sex show. Before falling asleep, I vividly remember a blonde bombshell performing the most amazing stunts. I have often asked myself the question: 'How can anyone fall asleep in a live sex show?' It seems impossible.

On the flight home, I remember Farquhar MacRae playing his fiddle at 32,000 feet, which may be some kind of record. All ended well, however, when the Iceland Air jet touched down safely at Glasgow Airport.

Copenhagen became a favourite destination for us, and we played there many times. One of the funniest incidents, which caused much hilarity, took place in a night club, on another trip to the Danish capital. It was the usual setup; a ha'penny stamp dance floor surrounded by tables and chairs, with low lights and throbbing music. We were all sitting at a table, and right opposite us there was a table full of beautiful young girls. There was all the usual 'boy chat': 'You fancy this one or that one?' 'You fancy the brunette or the blonde?'. I took an awful shine to a blonde girl sitting in the middle of the company. I decided that I would ask her up to dance, and I remember fine that it was a slow number – 'Fats Domino' if I'm not mistaken. I went over and asked her to dance, and she was very charming and got up immediately. Well, my God, she got up all right. When I stretch myself to my full height, I am five foot six inches, but when I looked up, without a word of exaggeration, this beautiful girl must have been all of six foot six. It must have been very comical, watching us doing a slow, groovy dance together in the middle of the floor. The top of my head was resting between her breasts, and she kept patting me on the top of the head. The boys were falling off their seats laughing at this amazing scene. I kept coming up for air, and then I would snuggle my head between her breasts again, as it was the only place it would go. Whenever a number came to an end the done thing, in those days, was to stay up for another, but I just couldn't get off quick enough.

About this time we took many entertaining trips abroad, but on one of these sojourns I developed a fear of flying, which has never left me to his day. It prevents me from even flying to Balivanich Airport. It is a fear of crashing. This phobia has been a major drawback in my musical career, having declined so many invitations to travel the world playing music. It has been very frustrating indeed. Having said that, had it not been for my fear of flying, I may have missed out on a lifetime of touring Scotland, and the Highlands and Islands in particular, so I suppose I have no regrets whatsoever.

My favourite country to visit has always been Ireland. I have made music in almost every corner of Ireland, north, south, east and west. It's a funny thing, but I have always found that the major cities, like Dublin and Belfast, are not really my cup of tea. In fact, I have always found the eastern seaboard very different to the west, although I have had some wonderful nights on that side of the country too. It's a wee bit like Scotland in many respects.

A number of years ago, the Scottish president of the Pan Celtic festival, Allan MacColl, invited me over to play at the Scottish ball, which was part of that year's festival, being held in Galway. The festival takes place in a different town in Ireland annually. It is a gathering place for all the Celtic nations, and is often a fairly elaborate affair. I would have been present for the first time in 1990, and have attended it faithfully every year since. The festival has taken me to Galway, Ennis, Tralee and, most recently, Kilkenny. I have always found the main action, the culture with which I can associate, in the west of Ireland; from Donegal down to Cork. All these areas, Galway, Connemara, Sligo, Dingle Bay and Tralee are very similar to the West Highlands of Scotland. It is like drawing a line down from Cape Wrath to Campbeltown.

The culture is similiar. The Gaelic language is still very much to the fore, and the music is very much in line with our own West Highland, ceilidh, Celtic music. I feel very at home and at ease with the people in the west of Ireland; there is a certain affinity between Highlanders and Irish people anyway. We have always really been linked in music and song. The west of Ireland is really the home of the ceilidh band sound. You can distinguish an Irish ceilidh band from all the rest by the music that they play. It has beat, it has lift and it has that unmistakable ceilidh band sound. It breaks my heart when I hear groups in Scotland calling themselves ceilidh bands. They are a million miles off the mark. They may think that they are playing ceilidh music but the way that they play it, and the general sound, suggests to me that they are just a glorified Scottish country dance band playing a wee bit faster.

14
Rolling in the Isles

I suppose, in all honesty, I have spent most of my life touring 'overseas', if one considers my travels in the Hebrides. I have always enjoyed a special relationship with the Hebrideans, and the people of the Western Isles in particular. I suppose this could be put down to a shared Gaelic heritage. I always look forward to touring in the islands, each one having its own distinct character and flavour. No two trips have ever been the same. You just don't know what is round the next corner.

I remember once, my own band was making for a big dance in Portnahaven, on Islay. The lead guitarist I had at the time – John Hamilton was his name – was engaged to a young lady from Islay, whose father was the minister there. It would be around 1963.

The band left Glasgow and headed for West Loch Tarbert, where the MacBrayne's boat the *Locheil* was berthed. That was the boat on the Islay run at the time. We left our car at West Loch (for we would be met on the other side) and took aboard the amplifiers and other equipment. Johnny Hamilton had his fiancée with him. She was going home and was going to present to her parents this dashing young lead guitarist, in his final year at university, where he was studying to become a chartered accountant.

We boarded, and somebody had the bright idea of going down to the bar for a drink, as all bands did in these days. Well, I have to say, the bar in the old *Locheil* was down in the bowels of the vessel, and it's the nearest I've come to what I imagine Hell to be like. The noise of the engines was deafening, and smoke: you couldn't see your own hand with the smoke. The booze: the tables were just full of it.

The place was packed with people. The five of us crept up to the bar and ordered a drink. I remember somebody mentioning that Fraser McGlynn and his band were on the other side of the bar. Now Fraser, from Tarbert, Loch Fyne, developed into one of the world's great dance band leaders, but was just on his way to becoming a big name at the time, and I'm sure that could also have been said of ourselves. We had heard of each other. Fraser was obviously aware that Fergie's band was on board, and we had been made aware that his band was on board. It was like a scene from the Wild West: eyeing each other up, and nobody giving an inch; Clint Eastwood at one end of the counter, and Lee Van Cleef at the other.

Halfway across on the journey, a round of drinks was sent over to our end of the bar, and the barman said, 'That's from the Fraser McGlynn band'. So, the gentlemanly thing was to reciprocate by sending a round of drinks back. We became like gladiators. They sent another round over, and we sent another round back. This went on for long enough, until Fraser McGlynn's drummer – Robertson was his name – came over to speak to my drummer, Mike Dowds. Eventually we were all drawn in as one band, and before we reached Islay everybody was completely legless. We were pissed to the eyeballs.

I remember coming off the ferry with my accordion and an amplifier. It was a beautiful afternoon. The minister and his wife were there to meet their daughter and future son-in-law. She came off first, closely followed by Johnny Hamilton, who was being helped off the ferry by two deck-hands, his legs dragging behind him.

The poor girl said, 'This is my fiancé.'

The minister turned on his heels, and away he went in his car, leaving them there; and really, that was the end of the romance. That was my first experience of Islay, and one I will never forget.

We got onto a bus when we arrived at Port Ellen and headed for the dance venue, which was down in the 'Rhinns', Portnahaven Hall. We were duly booked into our digs, where the main object of the exercise was trying to sober ourselves up before ten o'clock and the start of the dance. What I remember well about this was that they were loading tea and coffee into us all evening.

So, when we arrived at the dance the organiser said, 'Goodness me Fergie, they told us you were all paralytic.'

'Och,' I said, 'it's amazing the rumours that go round. Look at us: we're just bang on the ball.' And we were bang on the ball. We played a blinder at the dance; we made sure of it.

We got back to the digs in the early hours of the morning. As usual, after playing all night, we were starving. We looked around, and there in the pot was a magnificent roast. This was our Sunday dinner, of course, that the old lady we were staying with had prepared. 'Oh,' I said, 'look at that. I think I'll have a wee bit of it. It won't do any harm.' So I had a wee slice. Then Mike Dowds and Johnny Hamilton – who was banned from his prospective matrimonial home – had a wee bit also. Noel Eadie had a piece, and Jimmy Yeaman had a piece as well. The biggest portion of all, however, went to my second box player Alasdair Clark; he nearly ate the lot. We all had another piece, and, bloody hell, we finished the roast altogether. There was nothing at all left of it. The poor woman, next day she had no dinner for us at all, at all. I remember that so well. She was so sympathetic to us, 'Och, you're just young boys, and I hope you all enjoyed it.'

That Sunday afternoon I met a man called Angus Curry. He was a piper and box player from Port Askaig. He was about the same age as me, and he had heard where we were staying.

He came over to see Fergie and said, 'We're going back over to Port Askaig, and take the box with you.' So, Sunday afternoon, away I went, and the drams were just flying around in the Port Askaig hotel. The bar was mobbed, and he had his box and his pipes, and I had my box.

We got awfully drunk of course, and he said, 'Do you know this Fergie? Do you know what you and I should do?' Then he said, 'I hear you get on awfully well if you join the Freemasons.'

'Oh that interests me great,' said I. 'How do you go about it?'

'It's dead easy,' he replied. 'There's a man that I know down in Portnahaven. He'll sign us on, no problem at all.'

Away we went, going to join 'the masons', as they called it.

They tell me there's a long rigmarole before you become a mason. You have to be recommended, it would seem. You cannot just go and join like that. We arrived at this poor man's house, and Angus said, 'There's the two of us here wanting to join the masons. Would you take us on?' The poor soul didn't know what to do with us. He explained that it took a long, long time before you even got near a masonic lodge. We were very down-hearted. We thought you could just join straight away. That was an amazing afternoon.

Escapades like our weekend in Islay were commonplace. In fact, in the early days of my first broadcasting band, our annual highlight was the Highland Tour, which would take place around the time of the Glasgow Fair in July. The Western Isles, in particular, would be overflowing with Hebrideans returning from Glasgow during the two-week trades holiday. It didn't matter what night of the week you held a dance, it would be full to bursting.

On one particular occasion we found ourselves playing at a dance in Portnalong on the Isle of Skye. It was a Thursday night, and we were to play a dance on Harris the following evening. This meant catching the morning ferry from Uig to Tarbert (on Harris) the next day. The dance in Portnalong was an all-nighter, and, needless to say, there were a few sore heads when we turned up at the ferry in Uig on the Friday morning. The ferry was the MV *Hebrides*, a vessel much loved and much missed by all who sailed on her. The crew – being mostly young Hebrideans and music enthusiasts – were our friends. Very rarely did we ever have to pay for our passage, and in return we would hand out complimentary tickets to our dances and hold impromptu ceilidhs on board. The band, as I recall it, was Mike Dowds on drums, Noel Eadie on bass, Johnny Hamilton on guitar and Farquhar MacRae on fiddle.

The boat sailed at 11 a.m. and we quickly made our base camp in the saloon bar, deep in the bowels of the vessel. I can remember drinking gin and tonic, as I had been told of its effectiveness as a hangover cure. It wasn't long before the cure became the problem. The bar was suddenly full of young Hebridean exiles, happy to be heading home for 'the Fair'. As the drink flowed, the inevitable happened. Instruments were fetched and a ceilidh – the likes of which you have never seen – began. It was like a scene from the Wild West. A packed saloon, thick with cigarette smoke, tables full of drams, young women squealing excitedly to the soundtrack of Fergie and his band, and all at 11 o'clock in the morning. It carried on unabated all the way across the Minch. In fact, such was our merrymaking that we failed to notice the ferry docking in Tarbert, and before we knew it, we were back where we had started in Uig. This was a terrible predicament. We now had no way of getting to Tarbert, as the only other sailing that day was from Uig to Lochmaddy in North Uist. It was then that fortune took a hold of proceedings.

The pier master in Uig, a gentleman by the name of Uisdean, shouted a message from the quayside to the skipper of the *Hebrides*, who was standing on the bridge.

'Tell Fergie and his band to stay on board and sail for Lochmaddy. They'll find out why when they get there.'

You see, the world was a very different place in those days, and communications were that bit slower. This, however, had its advantages. Word had spread in Harris that Fergie MacDonald's band had failed to make it ashore. Among the first to know were the girls who worked in the telephone exchange in Tarbert. They contacted the exchange in Lochmaddy, who in turn contacted the MacBrayne's office in Uig. When we arrived in North Uist we found that the dance we were supposed to play at in Harris had been moved to Lochmaddy Hall. If Mohammed won't go to the mountain, then the mountain will come to Mohammed, or Fergie.

I remember another occasion, a most amazing dance I attended on the island of Iona. In fact we were banned from Iona for many, many years after it. We were asked to play at a dance in the hall. This was before there was a hotel, a restaurant, a bar or anything on the island.

The *King George* used to call in three times a week; on Mondays, Wednesdays and Fridays, with trippers visiting the abbey. They used to be taken off the ferry and transported by tender. The *King George* would anchor just outside the bay, and boats were used to bring the passengers in and out. This was also the only means that the locals had of getting a dram for the dance on a Friday night. But, being a boat like the *King George*, the bar wasn't able to sell orthodox carryouts – half bottles and things like that – because they didn't have them. They would fill lemonade bottles and thermos flasks with whisky and vodka, for the people of Iona. Anyway, we arrived. It was a beautiful, beautiful night, and I had four of a band with me.

The dance started off fine, and the crowd was very generous with their bottles and flasks. We were drinking out of all kinds of receptacles; we didn't know what was in them. I'm sure it was like drinking a Molotov Cocktail, and before very long we all started to get very, very drunk indeed. You really had no idea how much you were consuming, when you went out the back and someone offered you a dram out of a thermos flask. You didn't know whether it was a nip or a glass.

Early on – it was before midnight actually – I happened to notice that my piano player was only playing with two fingers. His index finger of the left hand, and his index finger of the right hand. This was the first indication I had that he was on the way out. Very soon afterwards I looked round to find him slumped over the piano, sound asleep, with his hands outstretched. We carried on as best we could, when I noticed that the fiddler had at least two strings missing from his fiddle. He was still playing away quite the thing. Then the drummer fell completely backwards off his seat, and remained there, in a heap on the floor. Eventually, the fiddle-player (with one string left by now) collapsed, and fell asleep, leaving me on the stage, all by myself with the box. They tell me that all I could play, for a Barn Dance, Gay Gordons or a waltz, was the 'The Bonnie Banks of Loch Lomond' and *Cailin mo Runsa*. The dance was abandoned, and we were barred and banned from Iona. I never set foot on the island for twenty-five years. Eventually, after all that time, I reappeared on the island, with a new band obviously, and they couldn't get us back quick enough. We were asked if we could do a dance the following month.

There was something very exciting about playing in the Hebrides in those days. Each island seemed to come alive during the summer. We made sure that every year we would go on tour for three weeks all over the Highlands and Islands. This certainly wasn't for financial gain; it was just for the *craic* more than anything.

We used to kick off on Skye as often as not. The most amazing thing in these days used to be the ferry queues. Sometimes you would have to wait for hours. This was part and parcel of band life in those days, and was a good place to find out all the latest news on the music scene, as you used to meet all the other bands there as well.

When you arrived in Kyle of Lochalsh, for example, in the middle of summer, the waiting time would be a minimum of four hours. The queue of ferry traffic would be endless. In fact it was in a queue waiting for the Skye ferry in Kyle, that I first met Addie Harper and the Wick Scottish Dance Band. I had hero-worshipped that band all my life, and it was an amazing thrill to meet Addie Harper and Ewen Nicholson, both of whom became lifelong friends.

There was a barber's shop, if one can call it that, in Kyle. It was actually a little wooden hut at the top of the pier. The wee man that owned it used to give haircuts, obviously, but on the way out the door, you would give him a wink and a nod, and he would go into a box that he had yonder, and discreetly hand you a packet. You will have guessed by now that he was the local supplier of contraceptives, and all the bands heading west, that I knew of, used to call in there for a 'toothbrush' and a wink and a nod. It was absolutely amazing. All the bands knew about this, it was regular trade. That was always your first port of call before making for the Hebrides.

We didn't always make our way to the islands through Kyle though. Mallaig was often our preferred route, especially if we had to rely on public transport, as we often did. It never ceases to amaze me how these modern ferries on the outer isles runs can complete their journeys so quickly. It has certainly made life an awful lot easier for me. I can remember though, when this just wasn't the case.

Being a Glasgow-based band, we would have to catch the early morning 05.45 train from Glasgow Queen Street. We would travel by steam all the way up the West Highland Line, through Glen Falloch, Crianlarich, Rannoch Moor, a quick stop in Fort William before carrying on towards Glenfinnan, Arisaig, Morar and finally Mallaig several hours later. On reaching Mallaig, your first move was to hump all the gear and instruments down the pier, while dodging all the seagulls. More often than not, you would be met with an aerial bombardment before boarding the ferry.

The ferry which ran out of Mallaig in those days was the famous *Loch Seaforth.* She was an amazing vessel, with a wonderful crew, who would have crossed the Minch under any circumstances whatsoever. That says an awful lot for their seamanship. I had a good friend, Sammy Cameron from Acharacle, who worked on board at the time, and through Sammy we got to know the rest of the crew very well. There were legendary characters like 'Roddy the Cook' and 'Bimmy MacPherson' from Iochdar in South Uist. Bimmy used to work behind the bar and operated a form of barter system. There was a gentleman in Mallaig known as 'Harry Snap' who would often appear at the gangway with a box of kippers. Harry would be invited down to the bar, where Bimmy would trade the kippers for whisky. Sammy Cameron immortalized many of these wonderful people in a song which he penned himself. If my memory serves me right, I believe the words went something like:

My name is Sammy Cameron,
I work aboard a ship,
They call her the Loch Seaforth,
And she's really quite a heap.
We sail around the waters
Of the misty Western Isles
From Stornoway to Mallaig,
Every heather-tinted mile.

The barman's name is Bimmy,
He's a pirate of the sea,
A pint is two and tuppence,
But he charges five and three.
The stewardess is Mabel,
A Sgitheanach is she,
And if you're very naughty,
You can catch her dimpled knee.

There were many more verses and it was always sung to the tune of 'Mary-Ann MacRae'.

The journey was always a long and hazardous one, up through

Top. On the road, early 1960s: Alastair Clark, Noel Eadie, Mike Dowds, Calum Kenmuir and Fergie

Bottom. Fergie standing by Loch Maree, late 1960s

FERGIE
MacDONALD

Opposite. On stage at The Highlander's, early 1960s: Gordon Fraser, John Hamilton, Mike Dowds, Noel Eadie and Fergie

Top. Copenhagen, late 1960s: Farquhar MacRae, Mike Dowds, Noel Eadie

Bottom. Fergie's parents (John and Mima), early 1970s

Top. Scotland shooting internationalist, with 14 Scottish caps, pictured here with Keith Bond (England captain)

Bottom. The Clanranald Hotel

Opposite. The trappings of fame and fortune: Fergie outside the Clanranald

FERGIE'S BAR
HOTEL & RESTAURANT

Top. Fergie entertaining guests in the Clanranald

Bottom. Fergie with Irish button-box wizard Sharon Shannon

Top. On tour in the Hebrides, 2000

Bottom. Fergie and Groupies, Berneray Hall 2000

Top. Fergie and Farquhar MacRae, an inseparable team for almost half a century: Alan Savage, Ian Kennedy, Farquhar MacRae, Fergie

Bottom. Fergie with Castle Tioram, home of the Clanranalds. Fergie's family roots go back to the Battle of Sheriffmuir and of course the Forty-five Jacobite rebellion

Kylerea, calling in at Kyle of Lochalsh, then on to the north end of Skye, before crossing the Minch, which could be beautiful, but could also be devastating. The return journey on the *Loch Seaforth* was always the one that we would enjoy the most. The boat would leave Stornoway harbour just after midnight. We always caught it on a Sunday night, just after the end of the Sabbath. Once we were half an hour out, the bar would open. Now this boat would be at sea all night, until about eight o'clock in the morning, when it would arrive back in Mallaig in time to catch the Glasgow train. This was an epic journey. It never failed to live up to our expectations.

You would board the boat, hang about for half an hour until the bar opened, and then the ceilidh would start. Obviously, being musicians, we were right in the middle of things. The merriment would continue all night long, until the boat berthed in Mallaig next morning. It was a real hardcore session, drams and music until people could take no more. There would be tunes hammered out on pipes and accordions, Gaelic songs that you had never heard before, people throwing each other round the bar as they danced their hearts out, girls screaming. It was just an incredible scene. I only wish that I could have videoed or photographed it. What I do have are these wonderful memories that I'm sure will never leave me.

When you finally arrived in Mallaig, there was nothing for it but to board the train and be miserable for the next six hours until you reached Glasgow. It was awful, sitting on hard seats, nursing the obligatory hangover, as the train puffed its way south. Anyway, that was always for the end of the tour and never figured in our thoughts all that often at the start of the three weeks.

We would often start our tour with two nights in Skye (usually Portnalong and Uig), before heading for the Outer Hebrides. I recall being booked for a dance in Uig one night. The dance was from ten o'clock until one in the morning. We decided to stop in every bar between Kyle of Lochalsh and Uig, and we ended up being two hours late. We didn't arrive at the hall until midnight. By the time we got there the hall was packed, and what a cheer we got when we walked in! You would have thought we were the Rolling Stones. Modestly, I have to say that we probably were, in the eyes of the young people of Uig at that time. Rather than finish at one, we gave them two hours extra, so that it went on until three in the morning. Now, all was forgiven. It was a very relaxed kind of affair. After the dance was over you would always end up at the inevitable party. There would be singing, and more whisky, everyone having a right good time.

On one of our first visits to the islands, we ended up in Ness on Lewis. This was to herald the start of my career as a composer, although I didn't know it until afterwards. We played at a dance first of all, which I will never forget. It was our first dance on the island of Lewis, as a band. Being Glasgow-based, we arrived at the hall at nine o'clock, to find the doors still locked. Ten o'clock came, and still the hall lay empty. We happened to see a little boy going past on a bicycle, and we asked him where the hall-keeper's house was. 'It's over there' he said, pointing along the road. It was after ten o'clock by this time, so we went along and found the hall-keeper, who was surprised to see us. 'You're very early,' he said.

He told us that he would be along with the key in a wee while, so we waited, and waited, and waited, until eleven o'clock. There was still no sign of him. At half past eleven, he eventually arrived with the key, by which time we were convinced that we were at the wrong venue. We thought that somebody had made an awful mistake. Anyway, the hall was opened, and we began to set everything up. Soon enough it was midnight, and not a living soul in the hall. We decided we might as well pack up our gear and head for home. Just as we were about to start dismantling the set-up, two ladies arrived and took positions at the door. It looked as if, at long last, something was going to happen. Something indeed; in fact I will never forget what happened. Within ten minutes the hall was mobbed. You couldn't even dance. It was far too full. I have never seen a venue fill up so quickly in all my life. We soon learned that nobody bothered going to dances in that part of the Hebrides until between midnight and one o'clock.

We really went for it. We played until four o'clock in the morning, at which point we were invited for a drink in the local 'bothan'. The boys had heard of this place, but believed it to be nothing more than a myth. I knew differently. A 'bothan', as you now know, is an illegal drinking den. Usually a thatched shed or some but and ben, where the whisky runs free. We were very excited at getting an invite, and along we went. Well, this really opened my eyes anyway. There it was, at half past four in the morning, going full swing, with a peat fire you could have roasted a bull on. The heat was incredible, everybody had sweat pouring off them. Whisky, like water, running all over the place. Everybody was smoking roll up cigarettes, Gold Flake and full-strength Capstans all the way. It was the most amazing scene. There was never any money shown at all, at all, in case of raids or anything like that. The place was frequented by the cream of Highland and Island gentlemen; bad eggs were not allowed. This was a highly select company, the pick of the area. In the middle of it all, nature called, and I went outside to relieve myself. Before I knew what I was doing, I found myself sprawling about in the most enormous mountain of empty cans and bottles. I actually slipped in the middle of them, and could I get myself up? Somebody saw me rolling about, and came and hauled me out of this nightmare. To cut a long story short, the next morning the first tune that I had ever written began to form in my mind. I called the tune 'Ness Bothan', and that is a tune that has become very, very popular. Most musicians involved in traditional music are familiar with that tune.

Still on the subject of bothans, I remember another time I was up in Ness. It was the same sort of procedure as before, although by then we were used to it. I had a young lady with me, who was from the mainland. Women weren't really allowed in the bothans, but somehow they made an exception on this occasion. It was the early hours of the morning, with the sun rising over the North Minch, looking towards Cape Wrath. It was a beautiful, beautiful morning.

Being a young, virile band leader, I decided to 'take the air' for a minute or two in the company of a young lady. The bothan itself was in a very open sort of area, with a thatched roof. However, one could step onto the thatched roof from the side of the wall which ran past the building. We climbed on top of the thatched roof and made mad, passionate love on top of the bothan. That is one of my more affectionate memories of these wonderful drinking dens.

We were heading for Castlebay, Barra, the very next day. This involved leaving our vehicles at Rodel, in Harris, because we were returning in about three days to play in Tarbert. Ferries weren't so well linked up back then, so the only way to get to Barra was to take a small ferry from Rodel to Newton, in North Uist, and then hire a vehicle to drive all the way down through the Uists to Ludag. From there we caught a ferry to North Bay, in Barra. I think we must have picked the wildest day that I ever remember.

We were, first of all, in an open boat from Rodel to North Uist. Luckily the skipper had a tarpaulin, which we were able to spread over the amplifiers. There were friends of ours waiting at Newton Ferry in North Uist when we arrived, and they offered to drive us all the way to Ludag, in South Uist, to save us hiring a car. When we arrived at Ludag we were met by Neil Campbell, OBE. By this stage, the gale must have been near enough storm force ten, but Neil Campbell would go under any conditions. It would have taken a hurricane to stop him. I suppose that is why he received the OBE. He was one of the finest seamen I have ever met, and a true Highland gentleman.

'Will we make it Neil?' we asked.

'Ach well, we'll give it a try,' he replied.

If Neil Campbell said that he would give it a try, he meant that he was going. Off we went, and, without a word of a lie, we were all afternoon between Ludag and North Bay. He was dodging from island to island, trying to avoid the worst of the weather. The waves were breaking over the gunwales of the boat, and soon we noticed that the amplifiers were swimming in sea water. Eventually we made it over, and headed for Castlebay, where we were met by Father Angus MacQueen, who became a personal friend of mine over the years. Father Angus set us up in digs, and then left us to get out of our wet clothes and prepare for the dance that night.

When we arrived at the hall we set up the amplifiers and switched them on. All we saw was a puff of blue smoke and flames, and there we were on Barra, with at least a crowd of 300, and no amplification to speak of. Touring can turn very, very nasty sometimes. People remember your good nights, but all it takes is one bad one for the war cry to change to 'Fergie's band was hopeless last night'. Ninety-nine per cent of the public do not realize that circumstances have a lot to do with it. We started playing, but obviously with a crowd of that size, nobody could hear us. That meant that Fergie's band was bad news that night.

Anyway, the following night, Sunday evening, we obtained an amplifier from a local band to play at a dance in Northbay Hall. It is certainly a night I will never forget. The night started off fine and things were going well. However, we took it in turns to go out to the toilet. Every time you went outside, a half-bottle was stuck in front of your nose, so we soon cottoned on to this. Three would remain on stage, and one would go out, come back in, and then relieve another band member, and so it went on. The whole thing became really quite ridiculous, although it finished off as a most wonderful night. There were many calamities along the way, and I am often mindful of the old saying: 'You're only as good as your last performance'. It is very true, and can be applied to dance bands, football or shinty teams, anything really. People always forget the good ones and end up slating you if your last performance has not been up to scratch.

On another occasion, we were invited by Father Angus to play at the usual Sunday night dance, again in Castlebay Hall. These dances tended to be mobbed, and this night was no different. It would be no exaggeration to say that the whole island seemed to be at the dance.

The ferry was due to leave Barra for Oban at one o'clock in the morning. We knew that things were going to be a bit tight, but as the hall is only a hundred yards from the pier, we decided that we would be able to finish our last dance at quarter to one, pack the gear in five minutes flat and be on the ferry before it sailed. We counted on having a few helping hands at the dance to help us achieve this. Along with our 'big gear' such as amplifiers, speakers and instruments, we would always carry a tartan bag, which contained all the leads, without which the PA system could not work. It also contained equipment of vital importance, like microphones. Now, with all the excitement of us trying to catch the ferry, the pier in Castlebay was black with people helping us with our gear, and cheering us off as if we were the Beatles or something. We were out on the deck playing things like 'We're no awa tae bide awa', and there was waving and cheering, joy and sadness. Anyway, we got away safely and our attention soon turned to our Monday night engagement, which was in the village hall in Plockton. We arrived the next night and were greeted by my old friend Charlie MacRae (C.M. MacRae), who was 'Mr Plockton'. Charlie was the hall secretary, and we had the usual chat about where we had been and how things had been, while the boys were taking in the gear and getting it set up.

It was at this point that a terrible realization dawned upon us. Not a word was spoken, but everyone suddenly looked at everyone else. I remember looking at Noel Eadie, who looked at me. We knew fine what was going through the other's mind. Where was the tartan bag?

In all our excitement and euphoria it had been left on the pier in Castlebay. Now, there we were with a stage full of amplifiers and speakers, without any leads, extension leads or microphones. What a predicament! Luckily, Charlie MacRae knew a local electrician, and he also knew where he could get his hands on an old microphone, which resided in a box at the back of the hall. The electrician came as soon as he was called, and somehow he got wires and matchsticks and managed to rig up some form of amplification. It worked, but only just. The sound must have been terrible. It was definitely one of our worst-ever gigs, bar none. The next day, the news was all over the west, 'Fergie MacDonald's band was in Plockton last night and the dance was terrible'. 'They were awful'. 'They must have been drunk'. We met with all the usual lines that are reserved for the band that doesn't quite match the expectations of your average punter. There we were, we had left Barra to the sound of cheers ringing in our ears, and one gig later our reputation was in tatters.

Highland and Hebridean tours were always logistical nightmares. As a touring band, you had to be able to rely on whichever mode of transport you were utilizing at a particular time. Unfortunately, reliability was often a luxury we couldn't afford. In fact, sometimes, our transport's lack of reliability was positively life threatening.

On one occasion we were looking to buy some form of transport to take us round on our annual Hebridean tour, when I heard that a very dear friend of mine, Allan MacPherson, from Ardtoe, was selling an old van which he kept outside his house for spares. Allan had intended to sell the van to somebody else to use for spares, and was a bit perplexed when I asked him if he thought the van would see us through a three-week tour of the Highlands and Islands. Allan MacPherson was a pretty good mechanic, and agreed that it was probably, at best, debatable. He eventually sold us the van for a nominal fee of ten shillings, which in today's money would be fifty pence, and off we went on our three-week summer tour. The van would go all right after a fashion, running all the time on two cylinders. As long as you didn't have to go up any hill at all, it would run along quite the thing. This was, of course, not an option on a Highland tour.

We set off from Glasgow, and started the tour in Onich hall, where John MacInnes had booked us to play at a fundraising dance for Ballachulish shinty club. That went very well; it was quite a nice flat road most of the way from Glasgow. The next night we were playing in Kyle, and we discovered, somewhere around Invergarry, that the van, quite literally, would not go up any hill whatsoever. We had to develop a technique whereby the boys would jump out of the back and push, while I would keep the throttle to the floor.

Eventually we reached Kyle and played our gig. That was also fine, but we realized that things would be hotting up again, as our next engagement was in Garve. This meant many more hills and steep braes. We set off early the next day, as we wanted to allow time for all our possible exertions, and had made a mental note of possible trouble spots. We knew that we were coming to a big hill near Lochcarron, but as luck would have it, we saw two enormous German backpackers hitching a lift by the side of the road, and quickly decided to give them a lift, as we thought they would come in handy. It turned out that the boys had no English, but they soon caught on when the van started labouring on the very next hill, and they heard me shouting 'out, out, out', followed by the other band members disappearing out of the back doors in various states of panic. At first they thought we were on fire or something, but were soon adding their not inconsiderable weight to our efforts. After a few hundred yards' climb, we eventually reached the top of the hill and temporary safety.

Later on that same tour we were travelling from Stornoway to

Tarbert in Harris. Just before you reach Tarbert, you have to drive over the famous 'Clisham', a very steep hill and the highest in the Hebrides. The steering wheel was not angled like an orthodox wheel, but sat parallel to the floor of the vehicle, if you can imagine that. You had to lean over it as you drove along. Half-way down the Clisham, no brakes! They completely failed. The van was jumping and leaping all over the road. We were on the verge, we were off the verge. We were all over the place. By this stage, I was forced to stand at the wheel to try and recover some control, with everyone screaming and shouting in the back. How we reached the bottom of that hill in one piece, I will never know. We decided to cut our losses and ditch the van, before it ditched us.

Occasionally disaster would be waiting for us when we returned home from our epic tours. One particular example of this is worthy of note. At the time in question, my line-up was Alastair Henderson on second box and bass, Noel Eadie on guitar and vocals and Jay Dewar, from Strathyre, on drums. That was a very popular band, probably one of the best touring line-ups I ever put together. We were big, big hits all over the Highlands.

Alastair Henderson was sharing digs with me at the time, in Broomhill Drive, in Glasgow. We were on the second floor of a building which was owned by a man who professed to be a film star of some sort, though none of us had ever heard of him. He was probably an extra in something or other. He was certainly very strict, and would inspect all his rooms once a week.

Just before leaving for our summer tour, Alastair and I decided that we were going to make our own beer, and ended up filling more than a hundred bottles with our home-made concoction. We corked all the bottles up, reckoning that they would be just right by the time we came back from our tour. When we did eventually return after four weeks, who was waiting for us at the front door but our friend the film star (Mr Jackson was his name). He was very tall and distinguished looking, and had a piece of paper in his hand.

'This is for you and your friend, Mr MacDonald,' he said.

'Oh,' I replied, 'what is it?'

'It's a bill,' he said, 'and quite a bill!'

I looked at it and nearly dropped. It was a cracker!

What had happened was that, while we were away, all the bottles – every single one – exploded, and his ceiling, directly below our room, had caved in. It had become sodden with beer, which was dripping into his sitting room. His carpet and furniture were ruined. It must have happened in the middle of the night. He had obviously got everything seen to and valued, and had come up with this bill, which we could never hope to pay. In true Highland fashion, we packed our bags and left the scene of the crime in the early hours of the morning, and we never again set eyes on the film star from Broomhill Drive.

15
Loch Maree

I am sure that everybody who knows me would probably think that I 'made it' musically through playing the box, but in fact it never quite happened like that.

As you have read elsewhere, we were almost condemned to death by the BBC, who banned us from the airwaves, and by EMI, who terminated our recording contract. We were left in no-man's-land, musical nomads travelling the Highlands, making music. This, however, was all to change.

It all came about the day after we had played at a dance in the village of Lochcarron, in Wester Ross. Incidentally, I happened to meet a young gentleman called Neil MacKay at the dance. I didn't know him at this point, but when we came off the stage for a cup of tea, he went up and took a turn of playing the box. I remember hearing him playing this wonderful, two-part jig that I had never heard in my life before. When he came off the stage, I asked him what the chances were of him teaching me the tune. He said that when the dance was finished we would sit down and he would teach it to me. Sure enough, the dance finished around three, and we both sat down with our accordions. I remember that I had obtained a bottle of whisky from somewhere. Neil also had a bottle, as did many others, who sat down to listen. Neil played this tune over and over and over to me. I am not a music reader, and learn all my tunes by ear, which can be tricky after you have had a few drams. Eventually, by six o'clock in the morning, the tune locked in, and I have played it ever since. In fact I have probably been the instigator of many more people playing it. The name of the tune was 'Wee Todd'.

Anyway, after leaving the hall, we managed a couple of hours' sleep, and breakfasted, before leaving for Glasgow, to fulfil our weekly Saturday-night booking at the Highlander's Institute. Jimmy Yeaman, our fiddle player, had another reason for getting back to Glasgow that day. He had tickets for the international football match between Scotland and Brazil at Hampden Park.

On the way south, we called in at the Kintail Lodge Hotel for a reviver. Jimmy Yeaman wasn't to keen on this idea, and instructed us all to make it a 'quick pint'. 'Och, don't worry Jimmy, I'll have you at Hampden before three o'clock.' I said. It just so happened that the main road, from Invergarry to Kyle of Lochalsh, was being built at that time, and R.J. MacLeod, the firm who had won the contract, were working on the stretch between Cluanie and Kintail. When we entered the bar at Kintail Lodge, the place was full of workmen. One of them was a man by the name of Tommy MacKenzie, from Inverinate, whom we got to know very well. Tommy was in the middle of singing a song, which all the other men seemed to know, and were joining in the chorus.

One of my band members, Alasdair Clark, who was a schoolmaster in Oban, said, 'Fergie, are you hearing that? That will be the next Hiking Song.'

His reference was, of course, to the song made famous by Calum Kennedy, which was a huge hit all over the Highlands at that time.

When Tommy had finished singing I made my way over and asked him about the song. I wanted to know who had written it, and where it had come from. Tommy explained that he didn't know, but that a gentleman sitting at the other side of the bar, who was from Poolewe, had taught it to them all. We stayed until we had learned the tune, and then began picking up bits of words here and bits of words there. One o'clock came, two o'clock came, three o'clock, and we were still in the bar at Kintail Lodge Hotel, playing our instruments, and everybody singing this song. We left there just in time to crawl into the Highlander's Institute at half past seven, and poor Jimmy Yeaman missed his football match after all my promises.

The week after that I had a week's holiday, and I wanted to find out who the writer of the song was. So, to that end, I went all the way back up to Kintail and met the gentleman from Poolewe who had taught everybody the song. His name was Roddy. He was a digger-driver on the road. He gave me the name of a man in Poolewe, and told me to head up there to see if I could locate him. I went all the way to Poolewe and asked for Kenneth MacKenzie. I was quickly told that he was from there, but that he no longer lived in Poolewe. He was the head forester on a plantation outside Inverness, near Nairn. So I immediately left Poolewe and travelled to Nairn, where I located him in his own home. I knocked and waited for a reply. When he opened the door, I told him who I was, and he welcomed me in. I was able to establish that he himself had written the words and the music to none other than the 'Loch Maree Islands'. I asked him if he would have any objections to Fergie and his band recording it. He said that he would love that, so I went back to Glasgow with the real words and the tune, straight from the horse's mouth.

We began performing it at dances everywhere, for a Boston Two Step, and we all had a shot at singing it. I had two very good vocalists in the band at that time, Noel Eadie and Johnny Hamilton, so I had nominated them to sing it, but Noel said, 'Ach Fergie, what about singing it yourself? Go on, we'll back you up.'

We phoned up Thistle Records, and were invited down to their offices. They thought we were going to record an Eightsome Reel, or a Canadian Barn Dance, or something like that, but we had other ideas. We wanted to release the 'Loch Maree Islands' on an EP. Thistle Records were not keen at first, and hummed and hawed about the whole project. However, we assured them that this was a hit in the making, so they eventually relented.

I always remember that the guy in charge of operations at Thistle was a wee man called Mr Farquhar. He must have been about four feet tall. He owned this huge Alsatian dog which used to go bananas during recording sessions. He would end up having to drag the poor thing out to his car.

We recorded the 'Loch Maree Islands' with Fergie on vocals and backing from my own band. We added an instrumental or two on the other side of the EP, enlisting the help of that wonderful piper Kenny MacDonald, who played chanter along with my accordion. In all honesty, we never thought much about it until it was released, but not long afterwards, maybe a fortnight, I received a telephone call at eight o'clock in the morning from the record company.

Now, at that time there was a national hit parade which featured the likes of the Rolling Stones and Elvis Presley, but there was also a Scottish hit parade which included all the top artistes like Andy Stewart, Kenneth MacKellar, Monty Sunshine, the Clyde Valley Stompers, Jimmy Shand, you name it; they were all in it. I nearly dropped the phone when I was told that we were top of the Scottish charts. I couldn't believe it. The voice at the other end of the line assured me that it was true, and that Thistle Records had had to work overtime to hammer out more copies of the EP. In a very short period of time it reached the 50,000 sales mark.

We realised early on that if you really want to make a go of things, you have to self-promote. When we recorded 'Loch Maree Islands', and the subsequent LP, 'Dancing at the Highlander's Institute' (which was a big seller also) there were very few, if any, local radio stations to give you any airplay. In fact, there was only really the BBC, and we had blotted our copy-books as far as they were concerned. Nowadays, new releases get fired out by all kinds of radio stations, but at that time there was only really the one, and they certainly weren't into playing requests.

The first commercial station to burst onto the scene was a pirate station by the name of Radio Caroline. Everybody used to tune into this, because it gave people what they wanted, which is something that the BBC could never have been accused of at that time. You could phone in, or write in, and they would play your requests for you. It gave rise to many other pirate stations, most notably, in our case, Radio Scotland.

Luckily we knew one of the Radio Scotland DJs fairly well. His name was Jack McLaughlin, a young man with the gift of the gab. Jack was to become one of our top radio presenters, but at that time he was very much like us, trying to make his mark. Radio DJ culture was just in its infancy in those days, spurred on by the rise of pop culture. It was a new craze, which catapulted the likes of Alan Freeman and Tony Blackburn to household-name status. We considered ourselves, as a Scottish dance band, very fortunate to have an ally in Jack McLaughlin, who would present programmes like 'Scottish Hour' and 'Irish Hour' for Radio Scotland. He was very good at churning out Scottish and Irish dance music, and our music in particular.

Although we knew him pretty well, we were still a young band looking for stardom, and weren't averse to using one or two underhand tactics to make sure of airplay. Whenever we were in Lewis or Harris, Durness or anywhere for that matter, we would send him postcards, supposedly written by someone else, requesting a track from Fergie MacDonald's latest album. The postcards would read something like:

> Dear Jack,
>
> Please could you play a track of Fergie MacDonald's band? Something off the new album would be great. I particularly like 'The Loch Maree Islands'.
>
> Yours truly,
>
> Willie John MacPhail.

There were many pseudonyms used, but Willie John MacPhail was one of the favourites. We would tune in every week and hear our own postcards being read out: 'They are the most wonderful band in the world' etc. You know, it wasn't long before we didn't have to write any postcards at all. Suddenly there were hundreds of postcards making their way to Radio Scotland. Such is the power of suggestion!

We were just like any other young group though. We got up to all the dodges, and at times they paid off. Radio Scotland was a good example of that. We actually started to get plugs on Radio Luxembourg after that, which also proved to be a good launching pad.

Nowadays everything is different. You cannot move for radio stations. Every locality seems to have its own independent station. This is another subject on which I tend to blow hot and cold. People are obviously trying their best, but my own feeling is that there should be some form of training open to any prospective local radio presenter or DJ. Many people on local radio come across as being amateurish, and this could be avoided through proper training and advice. I reckon something must be done. Many of the presenters that I hear are found to be sadly lacking. They are grammatically incorrect, unintelligible and often colloquial in their use of language. You may take the attitude that community radio is the people's radio, and therefore speaking the people's language is acceptable. I do not subscribe to this theory at all. It is up to broadcasters, both local and national, to set standards in spoken language.

Having said that, local radio is a wonderful medium, and would have aided our cause no end. We did, however, make good use of any broadcasting opportunities which were open to us. It certainly helped to make the 'Loch Maree Islands' a huge hit, and that, believe it or not, launched us all over Scotland as a dance-band unit. It catapulted us right to the top of the tree. We were in huge demand after that, and our vocals were featured much more heavily from then on. 'Rock 'n' Roll' was the big thing, and we were combining that with Scottish music. We were into Stones numbers, Fats Domino numbers, Little Richard, all these guys. We actually became what one might term, the Runrig of the 1960s. I have seen us trying to get out of Balivanich Hall through a fire door, with a police escort. They were trying to get us out the back of the building and away, to dodge the crowds. The amazing thing was that people always seemed to find out where we were, and the cars would start arriving before you could do anything about it. Before you knew it, it was party-time all over again. You cannot hide in small places like that. That was *craic*. We thought it was great. We were living the Rock 'n' Roll lifestyle.

There was a fashion at the time that the boys in the band were heavily into, although I myself wasn't. 'Freak Outs' they were called. You used to get the amplifier revved up to the point where the speakers would be screaming, blowing the roof of the hall with rock music. It caused mayhem; dances would be stopped! This was causing a lot of problems. There were a lot of eyebrows being raised. People were asking whether we were still a Highland ceilidh band or not. The vibes weren't really all that hot. Local ministers and community leaders were reckoning that we had a bad influence over the young people.

I was listening to a radio broadcast recently, where Ruaraidh MacDonald of Runrig was being interviewed. He was asked where his interest in rock music began, coming from a hotbed of traditional music like North Uist. How did he break into the modern idiom? He said that it all started when he was a youngster, in Balivanich Hall, listening to Fergie MacDonald's band. Maybe we didn't have such a bad influence after all.

These were the old days of the band. They were amazing days. We established a loyal fan base in the Gaelic heartland of the Hebrides and the western seaboard. It has remained so to this day. The people of the Highlands are our people, and as long as there is a demand, we will continue to play music in dance halls from Lairg to Balivanich, from Morar to Portnalong.

16
The Stammer

One of the worst handicaps a human being can have, barring a physical or mental handicap, is a stammer. My own started under the most amazing circumstances.

Probably about the age of six, I can clearly remember being on my knees, reciting the Lord's Prayer. Smack in the middle of the line 'give us this day our daily bread', I stopped, and the word 'bread' never came. Instead, what came out was 'ba, ba, ba, brr, brr, b'. The stammer was born. In those days, I reckon that the education system had a lot to answer for. Today, the slightest hint of a speech defect is picked up and treated immediately by specialists in speech therapy.

My primary school teacher was a woman of near retiring age and a real horror, called Jessie MacPherson; known far and wide as the 'Cailleach Mhor'. The worst nightmare was being forced to stand out in front of the rest of the class, and read a prose passage, taking two minutes to each word, while she carried on with her knitting. The highlight of this torture was the Christmas concert, held in Mingarry Hall. My party piece was reciting 'Little Boy Blue, Come Blow up Your Horn'. Why the hell could she not have given me a song to sing? Anyone who has a stammer will tell you that singing does not present a problem.

One day the priest arrived at the school and asked the Cailleach Mhor to nominate two boys whom she thought suitable to be altar boys. Guess who was first out of the hat. In these days, the Catholic mass was always celebrated in Latin. Can you imagine it? I couldn't say two words straight in English, far less Latin. During the mass, a great hush and silence is very evident, apart from the odd cough. Amid this deafening silence, I was aware of my school friends tittering at the back of the congregation. This hurt like hell!

I found that I would go to amazing lengths to get the word out. Walking along the road, your step would alternate from long to short, depending on how long it would take for a word to come out. Eventually, the person you are with begins to keep time with your step, until eventually you both end up in a bloody shambles. Thank the Lord that I didn't have to talk while marching in the army. Can you imagine the scene, and the sergeant major?

The most annoying part was when you got completely stuck on a word, and the person you happened to be talking to tried to help you. More often than not, he would say a different word from the one that you were trying to say. In your mind, you would be saying to yourself, 'you stupid bastard'. He was supposed to know what you were trying to come out with.

I remember I was once thrown off a bus going to school, between Corran Ferry and Fort William. Asking for a return from the conductor was like climbing Ben Nevis to a guy with a severe stammer. I opted to say nothing. A mile from Fort William, the ticket inspector came on, and because I had no ticket, he stopped the bus and told me that he had had enough of my type. I didn't even get the pleasure of saying anything to him, as even that would not have come out on cue. It was a desperate handicap.

During student life, whilst studying physiotherapy, classes and lectures were a nightmare. However, it was during my tenure in Glasgow that I decided to do something about it. In answer to an advert in some evening newspaper, I made an appointment with this lunatic quack, 'Dr Jason Budd', who claimed he could cure a stammer. His fees were extortionate. His cure was, amazingly, to shout the word 'ha' at the top of your voice, at hourly intervals, irrespective of where you were. One had to shout 'ha' ten times in quick succession. He reckoned that this strengthened the vocal chords and built up some idiotic form of self-confidence. Really, it was quite hilarious. I often laugh when I think about it now. You would be shouting 'ha, ha, ha' at the top of your voice in subways, public lavatories, dance halls and in your digs, even up the mountains while shooting stags.

I recall once being on a train travelling between Edinburgh and Glasgow. A man sitting opposite me obviously had a medical problem pertaining to wind. It was causing him obvious discomfort. I think he farted all the way from Waverley Station to Glasgow Queen Street. En route, my time had come for my ludicrous performance, and I shouted out 'ha' ten times. He confronted me with the choice phrase, which I will always remember: 'Listen, Bugger Lugs, are you trying to take the piss?' Once again, I opted to say nothing.

Like many people with a similar affliction, I always found the telephone a nasty piece of goods. Luckily, more often than not, you were on your own, and you could use all your tricks without anyone seeing you; talking on the in breath, running out of breath and still talking (a real favourite), and stamping your feet. Turning your face and mouth through the most disgusting contortions also works a treat. After years of working at it, I am not totally cured, but at least I can manage to carry out a near normal conversation. As one lady put it: 'Fergie has a delightful little stammer.' Fair do, I'll settle for that. My greatest fear was that one of my family would be landed with it, as they reckon that it can be hereditary. Thankfully, it seems to have bypassed my children. I suppose, in one sense, it has certainly given me a stamp of identification. Not one that anyone would wish to have, but strangely enough, it seems to be a part of me, and I accept it totally. At first I hated it so much, but now, to be honest, I throw in an occasional 'buh, buh, buh', just for the *craic*. It wouldn't be me if I didn't.

17
Suas Leis a' Ghàidhlig

I have always been very thankful that Gaelic was my first language. I had no English whatsoever until I went to school. Even yet, at my age, there are times before speaking when I think in Gaelic first. This is sometimes a very peculiar situation. When you think in Gaelic first, your sentence in English may not always sound quite right, as you are doing a direct translation. This does not always work terribly well.

The Gaelic language has helped me immensely throughout my life. I can state, quite categorically, that over 90 per cent of my truest friends are Gaelic speakers. There seems to be some bond. It all links up with your culture and heritage, sharing almost the same ideas. I am very thankful that I was brought up within Gaeldom.

It helps very much musically. I would almost go as far as to say that my music revolves around Gaelic language and culture. There are so many tunes; reels, marches, jigs, strathspeys, etc, that have Gaelic origins. And really, as I always say, unless you speak Gaelic and understand what the words are in most of these songs, there is no way that you can get it right. You might think that you are right and be able to mimic it, but really you are a million miles away from it. The greatest examples of this are Gaelic waltzes and slow airs. I have always tried to put the words in my music, the way the songs are traditionally sung.

In my younger days in Moidart and Acharacle, the non-Gaelic speaker was a complete oddity. He was the butt of local humour. Unfortunately, nowadays, the wheel has turned, and the Gaelic speaker has become the odd one out. Moidart has completely changed culturally. The crofting community has more or less disappeared.

There was a time (not so very long ago) when as far the eye could see, croft after croft would be filled with haystacks and corn rigs in the months of August and September. It was really breathtaking. Most of the crofters now are no longer indigenous local people. In my book they are not crofters. The communities are not what they were. These days, most of the local crofters are at each other's throats. This happens for many reasons: fences, boundaries, common grazing areas, etc. This is the down side of the modern-day incomer crofter. In my youth, this was not the case. The Moidart that I grew up in was a very different place. We were brought up to be very proud of being from Moidart and, as Gaelic speakers, we were particularly proud of our own unique dialect of the language. I know that the Gaelic dialects distinct to Moidart, Morvern and Ardnamurchan are considered to be very pure. Mind you, I am sure that people in other areas would contest that, believing their own dialects to be of a higher standard. They are entitled to their opinion, as I am no linguist. I have, however, been around all the other Gaelic-speaking areas, and what I can say with some degree of certainty is that my own Moidart dialect is fairly easily understood by all. It does sadden me greatly though that this dialect, along with the language, may one day die.

Measures have been taken though to make sure that this does not happen. We have a Gaelic medium unit at the local primary school, and Gaelic will be very much to the fore in the new Ardnamurchan High School. Once more though, I notice that many of the children attending the Gaelic medium unit, or studying the language in the new high school have been forced to do so by their parents. Maybe the parents now believe it to be the in thing. Maybe it doesn't matter. Maybe the important thing is that these children are learning the language in some shape or form, and may be used to promote and project our culture. That is probably the only future that it has, at least on the mainland. The days of both parents in the household speaking Gaelic to their children are long gone. If the only way is Gaelic medium education, then so be it.

The *feis* movement has helped, but needs looking at big time also. My own feeling is that the Gaelic language should be far more a part of *fèisean* than it is at the moment. The route here really has to be through the tutors. There are very few Gaelic speakers teaching at *feisean*, and this is an area that has to be looked at very, very carefully. We have Gaelic-speaking musicians whose skills, I'm sure, could be utilised at the majority of *fèisean*. Their places seem to be taken by a lot of tutors who, in my book, leave a lot to be desired. A lot of them need tutoring themselves as far as I am concerned. Then again, maybe the powers that be at '*Fèisean nan Gàidheal*', the body which oversees all the respective *feisean*, should be held responsible for this. They should be looking more closely at the capabilities of individual tutors.

As far as the local *feis* committees are concerned, there are a number of them that need a fresh impetus also. These bodies are made up of very hard-working individuals, who give of their time freely, but at times maybe they need some new direction. It can often be very important to have a new perspective on things. I would like to see more young local people getting involved with these committees. Once more, it is up to the younger generation to get involved and take a more active role in the *feis* movement. Young blood may yet be the saviour of our Gaelic culture.

18
The Mod

National Mods were events that I only ever read about in the newspapers. I had heard so much about this unique festival of Gaelic music and song, but although a Gaelic-speaking Gael, the Mod was one area of which I had no first-hand experience. This, however, was to change.

In 1965, the Fergie MacDonald Dance Band were invited to play at the Largs Mod Ball, held in the Moorings Ballroom. The contract included a couple of spots at the grand concert, which featured all the main prize-winners, including the male and female gold-medal winners. The winners that year were Mairi MacArthur and John Murdo Morrison.

The ball, as usual, was a sell-out, starting about eleven o'clock, and finishing around three in the morning. We were very neatly turned out in black evening suits, black bow ties and white shirts. That night the band was: Fergie on lead accordion; Gordon Fraser on second box; Mike Dowds on drums; Noel Eadie on bass; Calum Kenmuir on piano; Farquhar MacRae on fiddle.

After the ball had finished, we all thought that was the end of our evening. However, while we were loading our gear into the car, parked beside the ballroom, who should appear but 'Pibroch MacKenzie', the famous fiddler from Tobermory.

'Hello boys, how about a tune?' he demanded.

Reluctantly, but with an audience by now standing around us, we all started to make music on the street. Within minutes, there must have been a thousand people round us, dancing and singing. The place went mad. Eventually the police arrived and decided to move us on, in the nicest possible way. Then it was on to hotel bars and pubs, ceilidhs everywhere. There would be a dram stuck in front of you, it didn't matter where you turned. There were girls everywhere also. Eventually a few of my band members, me included, and a bevy of beauties, ended up in someone's bedroom. Babes, Booze and Baile Cnocan, were very much the fashion by six o'clock that morning.

I must have woken up about eleven o'clock the next morning, and I can remember looking at the various bodies sprawled around this little room. Some were in beds, some were on the floor, some sitting on the floor; propping up the wall. I remember being most embarrassed, wandering around Largs, with my evening dress suit covered in little down feathers. What a give-away! I had also lost my accordion at some point, and it took a search party to discover its whereabouts. It was found in the late afternoon, behind a bar. Obviously, some kind understanding barman had saved it the night before. After regrouping in the late afternoon the band headed back to Glasgow, with splitting headaches, and played in our usual Saturday night venue, the Highlander's Institute. That was my first, but by no means my last, venture to the Royal National Mod.

I remember meeting up at a mod once with my old friend, that great singer and entertainer, Calum Kennedy, whom I admire as a man and as a performer.

Calum had been asked to sing, and he, in turn, asked me to accompany him. The problem was that I didn't know the first thing about keys and things like that, and Calum was so used to being accompanied by Will Starr, who knew every little nuance of Calum's performance, and never had to be prompted or reminded of a key or musical arrangement. Calum turned to me and asked, 'Do you know the song "Dark Lochnagar" Fergie?'

'Yes, kind of,' I replied.

'Well, give us an introduction, and just play wee bits here and there,' said Calum, turning to face his audience.

He told me the key as well, but I hadn't a clue what he was talking about, so the inevitable happened. I gave him an introduction in the wrong key, and the range in 'Dark Lochnagar' is colossal, as anyone familiar with the song will know. The poor man nearly passed out going for the high notes. He looked at me with the face of a man whose parachute has failed to open. Fair do to him though; being the great professional that he is, he plugged his way through it. The whole thing went all to hell, but he kept on going.

The Mod is really the annual highlight of Scotland's Gaelic scene. It can be looked upon as a festival, or competitions, or as a holiday for many Gaels who converge upon the different location of the mod each year. For others, it is a way of life. I know a man who has not missed a mod for thirty-eight years, and he doesn't even sing or play an instrument. In affectionate terms, it is referred to as the 'mating season of the Highlanders', or the 'Whisky Olympics'. Maybe that is a little naughty, but that is the way that many of our Lowland counterparts see it. In my view, it is a wonderful week for meeting old acquaintances and making new friends, and long may it continue.

When I look at the actual structure of the Mod though, with its different competitions and test pieces, I would have to say that, in my opinion, some areas need looking at. In the not-too-distant past, winning the prescribed song competition for the gold medal at the mod was really one of the most prestigious distinctions that any singer could attain. It was also a stepping stone towards stardom. Many young singers who won the coveted ladies' and gents' gold medals went on to become internationally known artistes in the world of entertainment.

Nowadays this seems to have changed, and the conveyer belt seems to have stopped. In the past, as I mentioned, it was a ticket to stardom. You were instantly on radio and television, and recording deals were thrown at you. You were very much in demand as an artiste to perform at concerts and ceilidhs all over Scotland – all over the world in fact. To be very frank, in this day and age the fact that you have won the gold medal at the National Mod cuts no ice whatsoever. The singers still work very hard to learn their songs, some spending a whole year just perfecting their pronunciation. Voice projection and all the other paraphernalia that go along with it are polished to a high standard also. Whoever wins it nowadays may end up on television that night, and then you never hear of them again. It is a one-off situation. They might be fortunate enough to sing at a few ceilidhs in their home locality, but that is about as far as it goes. It is very difficult to pinpoint where it has all gone wrong. My own view is that the powers that be at the Mod have got it all wrong. I would almost go as far as to say that the true winner of the National Mod should be the singer who wins the traditional gold-medal competition, as this has far more to do with our culture than the operatically influenced style of singing so prevalent in the mainstream gold-medal competition itself. Also, competitors in the traditional gold medal are not shackled by the restrictions placed upon them by written music, in the way that competitors in the mainstream competition are. This is not true Gaelic music as I know it.

This also reflects on a lot of the other competitions. Recently, I was adjudicating the accordion section at the Mod. The test pieces required in the syllabus were a traditional march, Strathspey and reel. There was quite a bit of controversy caused when I reached my verdict in each of the three competitions: junior, intermediate and senior.

After reaching my decision in the junior section, I was approached by a very angry father who said: 'I don't understand your form of adjudication at all. My son turned in a flawless performance there.'

'I know that,' I said.

'And yet you gave the medal to a player whose performance was not flawless.'

'That is correct,' I said. 'You have to look at the overall picture though. Does flawless playing necessarily contribute to phrasing, expression and the like? In short, does it mean that the playing is coming from the heart?'

'No,' said the irate father, 'but he never made any mistakes.'

'Sorry,' I said, 'that's not the way that I adjudicate.'

The winner had every attribute that I was looking for at the mod. He was playing his Highland, Gaelic music from the heart, and that's what counted for me. At the end of the day, that is what our premier Gaelic festival should be all about.

19
'One for the Pot'

Many traditions in the Highlands have only just died out. Being born and bred on a croft meant a very meagre existence. Going back over the centuries, the crofter, the indigenous crofter, was really kept under the heel of the local laird and his staff. Even now you will find that the landowner will very seldom employ a local man, irrespective of his capabilities. That just doesn't come into it. The old cliché is that the local cannot be trusted. He's an evil character who will poach you out of house and home. In olden times this may have been the case, but the operative word was 'survival'. People had to survive, and to survive you have to eat. There was little or no money or food. It was, as I have said, a very meagre existence indeed, living on a croft.

My first toy was a .303 Lee-Enfield rifle, brought home from the 1914–18 war. It was my father's own standard-issue rifle, and from the age of about four until eight, that was what I played with. My father was a marksman of the very highest calibre with a rifle. In his younger days he had been a gamekeeper, and at a very early age, I knew exactly the fatal spot for hitting a deer, rabbit or whatever. In fact, when I was ten years old, my father bought me a five shot, Sportsman-Five, BSA .22 rifle. I must have fired thousands upon thousands of rounds with that gun.

I still remember the first stag that I ever witnessed being shot. I was very young at the time, maybe about eight years old, and for some reason I awoke in the early hours of a July morning to see my father standing on a chair with his head out of the skylight window. He didn't know I was watching him. He was pointing a shotgun out through the window. The bang went off, and he turned round to find me staring at him. Rather than scold me and chase me off to bed, he told me to put on my shoes and trousers, and we went outside together to find a stag lying dead in the field. It turned out to be my first lesson on how to 'gralloch' or gut a deer. We then dragged it back to the house, and hung it up in the byre, where the hay and cows were kept.

It was an obvious progression onto shooting live game for myself, and my first kill was a roe deer. I remember it so well. I didn't shoot it with a rifle, but with a shotgun. My father taught me how to remove the pellets from a shotgun cartridge and refill it with three or four large, lead balls, which we called 'brusts'. These would be packed into the cartridge with candle grease. That was what I used to kill my first roe deer. I would have been aged about ten years old. It wasn't very long before I graduated further. At about the age of fourteen I learned the secret of dismantling your weapon, so that you had the butt in one side of your jacket and the barrel in the other. You could walk along the road and meet anybody without being suspected of carrying a weapon.

The favourite time for getting your dinner was dusk. Once you had located a beast, you kept your eye on it, and then just as night was falling, bang! We were always taught, even although it was dusk, that you only ever fire one shot. That was the golden rule. It didn't matter what the circumstances were, you never fired two shots, as anyone hearing a second shot would probably be able to locate you. Any gamekeeper hearing a shot would probably be able to pin-point your location from your second shot. That was the danger. The scene of the crime had to be left spotless too. Gamekeepers were very adept at spotting places where deer had been shot. Everything had to be cleared up or taken away. For this reason, it was often advisable to go poaching in twos. As often as not you would be miles away from home, so an extra pair of hands was always appreciated when taking the kill home. The beast would be split into hind quarters and front quarters, with hind quarters being the more desirable of the two, if you had to walk for any length of time. You would make a slit through the knees of the animal, which you slid your firearm through, and this would help to stabilise the load.

The other danger that you were warned about was wounded animals. Even a small roe deer could be a menace if you had not killed it outright. My father always taught me to keep a stone about the size of your fist handy. When you got near the animal, you would let fly and bring the stone down on its head. This was to make sure that it was dead. If you hadn't killed it, the blow would stun it sufficiently to allow you time to get the knife into its throat. This is tough stuff, I know, but I grew up in tough times amongst tough men.

Moidart was a very poor area after the Second World War. Ration cards were still on the go and food was very, very scarce. It was a real treat to have venison, rabbit, sea-trout or salmon on the table. I naturally developed into a young 'poacher', shall we say. There is no better word for it. My home, for many years, was never without venison, salmon, sea trout or wild duck.

The local gamekeeper was Allan MacColl, a real gentleman, who knew fine well that I was up to no good. But true to the gentleman that he was, he never pursued me in any way whatsoever. Although at the time I was always being very cagey, because you always feel that the gamekeeper is after you. Like many more young men, those times really taught me how to stalk game. If you are using a shotgun, you have to get in as close as thirty yards from your prey. That stands you in good stead for the rest of your life. You are then able to stalk with a rifle. It was instilled into us that we had to survive. I keep emphasizing survival. That was the key. At an early age, we all learned how to catch a fish, shoot a deer or snare a rabbit. That was the nature of our living. That was the name of the game. I was no different to anyone else.

The 'Mointeach Mhòr', the 'Great Moor' was between my house and Loch Shiel, and it was a regular occurrence during the summertime, when the fish were running, that I would nip out with some of my friends and catch one or two salmon. We had worked out that the fish would take roughly seven hours from the falls at Dorlin, before hitting Loch Shiel. We also knew that when the fish were moving up the loch, they would follow the bank line. We would leave the croft house at dusk (which was about eleven o'clock in the summertime) and walk through the 'Mointeach Mhòr' towards the loch. You had to know the route very, very well in the dark, or you would be in deep,

deep trouble with the bogs and quagmires. If you were careful, you would arrive at the loch side after about an hour of negotiating your way through the bog land. It was always a favourite spot, because you were well away from roads and the like.

George, one of my friends, used to swim out with the end of the net, and would tie it to a buoy, which was about twenty yards out into the loch. We usually allowed ourselves an hour to wait for some action, and, if lucky, you would eventually hear the fish hitting the net. We weren't greedy in the slightest. I have to emphasize that. When we knew that we had half a dozen or so, the net would be pulled back in, and off we would go, back over the moor, and be home before daybreak. That was always the way of it. Except for one night when we were caught by surprise. It must have been a very heavy shoal of big salmon. We saw them hitting the net, which nearly disappeared. We didn't know what to do. We eventually managed to haul it in, and must have had around thirty fish. Well, hauling a net with thirty salmon over moorland is not for the faint-hearted, I can tell you. We just couldn't do it, and there was only one thing for it. We found an old peat hag, and reluctantly we had to dump a lot of them. For the other side of this story was that there was no way that you could take home all these fish and dish them out to people who were not in the 'inner circle'; hence the terrible waste. There were no freezers in those days. We had to eat what we brought home, or share it with a few trusted friends.

One of these trusted friends was our local priest, Father Galbraith, and his dear housekeeper, Mary Woods. They were wonderful people, and were trusted as one of the 'inner sanctum'. The schoolteachers, incidentally, were also in league with us. That was how the fishing side of things went.

Luckily for us (and contrary to the normal rule of thumb) the two gamekeepers were local men. They were very, very strict (as they had to be) normally, but we knew that they were well aware of our escapades. Although gamekeepers, they had both come through the school of hard times, and they knew that it was really one for the pot. I admire them to this day for ignoring their well-founded suspicions. For that, I personally say thank you. Had they been outsiders, they would have been crawling to their bosses to tell them that they had caught the local poachers, for that is what we have been landed with in the Highlands all these years.

There were many more escapades on the fishing side of things. I remember one morning, heading away very, very early with a friend, to fish on Loch Shiel. Now Loch Shiel merges with the River Shiel. You have to pass about a mile of the river in order to reach the west end of the loch where the steamer used to be anchored.

It was an early summer's morning in June. We were going along the road beside the river, when we saw this huge fish moving in what is known as the 'Blacksmith's Pool'. It was about half past four in the morning, and we reckoned that the gamekeepers, Allan MacColl and Ronnie MacMaster, would still be in their beds, although it was still pretty chancy. 'I think we'll have a crack at this,' I said. The rod was up, but it was sea trout flies that were on it; 'Soldier Palmer', 'Peter Ross' and a 'Black Pennel', which were the favourite sea trout flies locally. There was no time to be wasted so I yanked off the tail fly and threw on a salmon fly known as a 'Jock Scott'.

Almost on the first cast, the fish was on, and we realised that we had underestimated its size. We thought it was about six or seven pounds, but it was much, much bigger. Away he went, and I could hardly control him with my wee sea trout rod. He had taken most of the line off the reel before I knew where I was. He soon reached the end of the line and snapped it, as I was using only six-pound breaking-strain gut, which would have been perfectly suitable for sea trout. I quickly rolled in the line and what was left of the cast. The salmon fly was gone and we decided to get out of there fast.

The most amazing thing happened though, and it is the first time that I have released this story, for obvious reasons. That summer, a guest (I even remember his name – Major Sanderson) was fishing with my dear, dear friend, the gamekeeper, Allan MacColl. I met Allan one day during the Major's fishing trip (he knew I was interested in fishing of course). 'You know Fergie,' he said. 'An amazing thing happened today. Major Sanderson was fishing at loch end, and he got a cracker of a salmon; a sixteen pounder, with a salmon hook in its mouth.' 'Well, well,' I said. 'Isn't that amazing Allan?'

'Yes,' he said. 'Another gentleman must have lost it some day.'

I agreed with his assessment of the situation, and slowly retreated before any questions were asked. That was one of the nicer stories, although I have to emphasize again that we were only after one for the pot.

Of course, we were into every devious means of catching fish that one can think of. Our particular favourite was a deadly weapon known as the 'otter', which is basically just a piece of wood with a number of hooks and lines attached. There are various types of 'otter', but our design was peculiar to Moidart, and was developed by a local priest in fact. The thing that makes the Moidart 'otter' different is the way that the keel is attached to it, and the way that the reins are attached. Also, a Moidart 'otter' only ever uses ten flies. You use it in a breeze, and guide it out onto the water like a kite. Before you know where you are, bang, you're into a fish. We used to use it a lot for hill-loch fishing and for sea trout on Loch Shiel.

Another weapon of choice was a spear, which would be used on our small local rivers during periods of drought. There was a blacksmith's shop in the area in those days, and 'Ronald the Blacksmith' had the technique of making very sharp spears, which you tied to a stick. These proved excellent for spearing salmon. We always managed to find our dinner when it came to fishing.

As the years passed, circumstances changed. My experiences had made me what you might call a pretty effective angler and stalker. I began to be offered legal shooting and fishing, and these became two of my main activities. I suppose I am the archetypal 'poacher turned gamekeeper'. I have had the pleasure for over thirty years of managing the deer on the Glenuig estate. This has given me tremendous satisfaction. It has been a privilege to manage the estate for the Clegg and Llewellyn families. There is nothing I enjoy more than throwing the rifle on my back on a cold, frosty, winter's morning, and heading to the hill for a hind. In October, one of my greatest thrills is hearing the roaring of a stag, and then stalking it. It is something that is in you. It is in your genes. My view is that you either have it, or you haven't.

Nowadays, I see so many gamekeepers employed by the landlords who, to put it bluntly, are butchers, bakers and candlestick-makers.

They come into this line of work because they believe that it is a good steady job. The landlords employ them often because they are incomers to the area, and their job is to keep their eye on the 'locals'. As I have said a lot of locals are branded dangerous people, who will wipe out the entire deer population. It is thought better to have a stranger looking after the interests of the laird. Thank the Lord that all landlords are not like this. Some do, of course, employ local gillies and gamekeepers, which pleases me.

I suppose that I developed my own legitimate shooting and fishing activities with my hotel in mind. It is a great selling point that we are able to offer a range of field sports to our guests, and every year we receive an ample quota of hunters and fishermen from all over Britain and Europe. I am happy to say that my son John has followed very much in my footsteps. He now handles that side of the business, and is kept busy all year round as a stalker and game dealer. It is funny, but I suppose John has been brought up on the other side of the fence. He understands the world of the deer manager and gamekeeper, as that is what I have been all his life. He is appalled when he hears of some of my poaching escapades as a young man. 'How could you do that Dad?' he asks. It's a funny old world isn't it? John is very highly thought of by most of the local lairds, landowners and estate managers. He goes very much by the book and is a responsible 'hill man'. It is because of this that he is held in such high regard. In a funny way, that makes me very proud.

I, myself have always tried to be very fair to local poachers since my defection to the other side. I can see the picture from both corners, having been brought up on the other side of the tracks. My early world was one where the crofter had nothing but the bare necessities, and poaching was a means of survival, so I can understand the plight of the ordinary poacher.

I have actually caught a number of poachers, and feel well able to differentiate between the ones acting out of greed and for financial gain, and those just seeking 'one for the pot'. Luckily, up until now I have never had any serious confrontations, and on more than one occasion I have turned a blind eye when I realised that the individual was only after a bit of venison for his Christmas dinner, or something like that. My problem lies with the commercial poacher. These are unscrupulous operators, who would sell you down the river for nine pence. They give not one thought to the condition of the deer and kill only for financial reward. Often they are poor shots, and one hears many horror stories of wounded animals being left here, there and everywhere. They are a world apart from the decent, honest poachers, amongst whom I learned my trade.

20
The Boys in Blue

The life of a Highland ceilidh band leader is often a strange one. When away playing at weekends, you could be, quite literally, anywhere. You could be playing in Wick, on Skye, in Berwick-upon-Tweed, Edinburgh, Inverness, absolutely anywhere. You get very used to travelling back to your own home in the Highlands at all times of the morning. This brings me on to the many, many times that I have been halted in the middle of the night (and during the day as well) by the police. I can also remember a time when commonsense policing was the rule and not the exception. There are so many stories concerning this very topic that it would be difficult to tabulate them all.

One that springs to mind happened when I was playing at a dance on the Island of Lewis. The band won a bottle of whisky in the raffle. There were only three of us in the band on this particular night, but we managed to polish off the bottle before the last waltz, which meant that, in normal circumstances, we wouldn't be able to drive to our digs. It so happened that the local policeman was at the dance. He was, shall we say, partaking of our win as well. There were also many more half-bottles flying around the dance. Eventually, somebody decided that it was time for us to head home to the digs.

I remember the policeman saying: 'We cannot let Fergie drive up to his accommodation in the state that he is in.'

I remember everyone agreeing, but Fergie was determined that he would do just that. A consensus of opinion was soon reached that if the policeman drove in front of Fergie, nice and slowly, with the blue light on, everything would be okay. Fergie would get home safely. That is exactly what happened. We drove at least three miles and he deposited us safely at our B&B.

The final chapter to that story is that thirty years later I was playing at a policeman's retiral party in Dingwall. His name was Ian Fraser and he had retired as an inspector. He wanted Fergie's band to play at his party. It was all high-ranking policemen and their wives that were there. In the middle of the night, this man approached the band and told us who he was.

He was a retired policeman, and he said to me, 'Fergie, are you aware of the fact that I'm the policeman that drove in front of you from a dance in Ness hall, with the blue light flashing, and got you home safely?'

I had always wondered who the policeman was.

His last words to me were, 'See, if we did that today, both of us would be locked up in the cells in Stornoway!'

There was another time that we were terribly late on the road. We were heading for Uig, on the Isle of Skye, to catch the Outer Isles ferry. We weren't sure whether the ferry was at half past three or four o'clock. There were four of us in the band and I had an estate car at the time. We were awfully late. We must have been at Kyle of Lochalsh around three o'clock. It was all a question of when exactly the ferry was sailing. If it was four o'clock, then we would just make it; if not, then we were really pushing it. I remember coming into Portree, which had a 30-mph speed limit. I know for a fact that we were doing sixty miles an hour – double the speed limit. Before I knew it, there were flashing blue lights behind us. They were right on my tail, with the sirens going, so I halted.

The policeman jumped out of the car and recognised me immediately.

'Fergie, God it's yourself! What on earth are you playing at? You're doing sixty miles an hour. I have to stop you. This is quite ridiculous. You could kill someone.'

'Well,' I said. 'We have to catch the boat to Uist, and we don't know if it is half past three or four o'clock.'

'Oh,' he said, 'Just you hold on one minute.'

He pulled out his radio and contacted head office in Portree, and he asked them when the ferry to Uist left Uig. They very promptly found out. 'Well Fergie,' he said 'You're really pushing it. But I'll fire on the light and the siren, and you drive behind me all the way out of town.'

He put the boot down and we were still doing sixty going through Portree. When we reached the sign for open speed, he flashed me along, gave me a big wave and was shouting: 'Hope you make it Fergie' as we sped off. That was amazing.

There have been so many incidents. The policemen have always been so nice and such decent fellows, and I have always found them to be of great help.

There was another occasion when we were playing at a wedding in the Croit Anna Hotel at Fort William. At that point I had been a few years off the booze. We packed up our gear after the wedding dance and made for home. At the roundabout at the railway station the gear in the back of the car started to move. So I had one hand on the steering wheel and one trying to sort the PA out. The police were sitting at the side of the roundabout and they obviously noticed this erratic driving.

Just like a flash, there they were, wee blue light on and sirens blaring. The flagged me down and jumped out of the car. The usual thing happened. I am so used to it now. One walks round with a torch, looking at licence discs and tyres, while the other one is firing in questions. They were two young cops and they didn't have a clue who Fergie was. One of them informed me that I would have to come with them into the back of the police car; they would have to take the matter further. They first of all asked me where I had been. I told them that I had been at a Highland wedding. Immediately you could see their eyes lighting up. It must have been manna from heaven. At last, they had nailed somebody, with a view to promotion probably.

'A wedding?' they enquired.

'Yes, a good going Highland wedding,' I replied. 'I'm a musician you see, an accordionist.' Well, this must just have thrown fuel onto the flames.

'When did you have your last drink?' they asked.

'I would reckon about nine,' I said.

'Ah come on,' said one of the policemen. 'That's four hours ago. You must have had something since.'

'No, no,' I said. 'You don't understand. Nine years ago!'

They still made me puff into the bag anyway.

It seems that when they went back to the police station, they were telling some of the old hands. One of the more senior officers, Angus MacDonald from North Uist, told them straight away that they had wasted their time. He knew that Fergie hadn't touched a drop in a very long time.

I remember once being at a shooting match. It was a Scottish international selection meeting in Elgin. While at the shoot, I was given the opportunity of buying, cheaply, 3,000 shotgun cartridges from a reputable dealer. That is a lot of ammunition, but I got it at a bargain price. On the way home I had to fulfil an engagement in the Carlton Hotel, Inverness, which meant that I also had my amplifiers and my accordion in the back of the car. The night went fine and I headed for home. But just as I was coming through Fort Augustus, at the bottom end of Loch Ness, my exhaust hit the road, and the roar of the car was suddenly like thunder. This was in the early hours of the morning, remember.

I crept through Fort Augustus, trying to make as little noise as possible, but I didn't get far before (and I was waiting for it) the blue flashers appeared behind me. Again, it was two young policemen, and they didn't know who the heck Fergie MacDonald was.

'You're aware that you're exhaust has gone?' said the first officer.

'Oh yes,' I said. 'I'm so sorry about this.'

The other policeman was walking round going through the usual checks and procedures.

The first policeman was still grilling me when the one doing the checks with his torch noticed that I had a car full of all sorts of things. I had to explain that the amplifiers and the speakers (which were all brand new) were mine, and that I was a musician. You see, these things were worth an awful lot of money.

'That's very expensive equipment you have there,' said the first officer. 'Would you mind opening your boot?'

Next I had to explain what my accordion was. The policemen found this very interesting and asked me what else I had in the car.

It was then that one of them discovered my shotgun.

'What the hell is this?' he asked. I explained that it was my shotgun and that I had been at a shoot. He didn't seem to care, and shouted over to his mate, 'Hey Archie,' he said. 'I think we're onto something big here. What are all these boxes?' he asked me.

I explained that this was ammunition.

'Good God!' he exclaimed. 'There must be 3,000 rounds here.'

This was amazing! He was writing all this down; 3,000 rounds of live ammunition, a shotgun, an accordion, amplifier and speakers.

My son John was just a wee lad at the time, and had left one of his toy golf sticks in the car. I remember one of the policemen picking it up and saying, 'I suppose you're into golf as well are you? And I suppose like everything else you don't know where it came from.'

'Oh I can explain everything,' I told them.

The policeman who had spoken to me first told the other one to take down my particulars while he made a quick call. He walked a short distance to his car, and I could hear him on his radio. He went through all the usual police jargon: 'foxtrot' and 'Charlie' and all this carry on. Lo and behold, it was Fort William police station that he was speaking to, and it so happened that there were two dear friends of mine on duty that night. This young cop was busy telling them about this guy that they had apprehended with all the gear in his car: ammunition, shotguns, accordions, you name it. There was even a fishing rod involved somewhere along the line as well. Somebody at the Fort William end asked for my name. 'It's Duncan Ferguson MacDonald,' replied the young officer. He then listened intently to his radio for a minute, before shouting over to his colleague, 'Ask him if he's better known as Fergie MacDonald.'

'Aye, that's me,' I said.

Well, it would seem that the police officers in Fort William were rolling about in stitches. It was then that a policeman with some seniority in Fort William came on the radio and informed the two young lads in Fort Augustus: 'This guy is an international clay-pigeon shooter, representing Scotland on many occasions. He is also one of our foremost musicians. Let him go!'

The young policeman came back from his car, and I shall never forget his words. He said, 'After further investigation, it would seem that my superiors have decided to let you go. But, my God, if it were left up to me, you would be straight into the cells right now! Away you go.'

It turned out that he was a young lad from Harris who had just joined the force. I actually got to know him quite well. Many a laugh he has had about that incident, and he still cherishes it as one of the great early moments in his career.

21
Alcoholism

I had my first drink of whisky around the age of fifteen, along with my first cigarette. If I remember rightly, it was down to our colourful art teacher at Fort William Secondary School, Miss Jamieson.

One Saturday morning, a few of the older boys from Greenhill Hostel (myself included), and some of her teaching associates were detailed to help Miss Jamieson flit. The manpower was divided between Gordon Square, where she had been staying, and Inverlochy, her new residence.

The hostel boys were busy emptying the furniture from the flat in Gordon Square into a waiting lorry. While the lorry was away, we found a bottle of whisky; three-quarters full. We all got stuck into the bottle and finished the lot, replacing the whisky with cold tea. It seems that a most embarrassing situation arose during Miss Jamieson's house-warming party. When all glasses were charged, her teaching friends were more or less forced to drink this concoction out of sheer politeness. Mind you, there wouldn't have been any sore heads the following day. There was hell about that!

The fly drinking continued throughout fifth and sixth year, especially at the school dances. The idea was to impress the girls who, we hoped, would think of it as a sign of maturity on the boys' part.

Two years of national service in the army helped the gradual process of building up one's capacity for alcohol. Pints of beer and cider were very much the order of the day. These pints with the boys around the pubs and clubs of Aldershot and London became regular weekend outings.

On completion of national service, it was on to Glasgow and an introduction to the world of entertainment. Being an accordionist, I began mixing in circles that were light years away from my sheltered upbringing in the Highlands. At Highland gatherings, society balls, dances, ceilidhs and concerts, pints were no longer the order of the day. It was more fashionable (and convenient) to drink whisky, gin, champagne and wine. I was quickly accepted socially in these circles, as my constitution and my ever-increasing capacity for alcohol meant that I was rarely to be found rolling around drunk. I could consume large quantities of whisky without showing visible signs of drunkenness.

As the years passed, the social drinking led to habit-forming drinking binges – and then, almost overnight, the realisation of dependency on alcohol. A very regular pattern soon set in, which went along the lines of playing at a dance on a Friday night, followed by the obligatory party. You would usually get to bed around seven in the morning, waking up on the Saturday afternoon with a headache and a hangover. The quick remedy was, is and probably always will be a stiff drink; in my case, a large dram of whisky. Just before performing again on the Saturday night, while still feeling rough, more drink would be consumed. That progression eventually led me to the stage where drinking became completely routine before a performance. This would be followed by more drink throughout the night, without ever going overboard.

Because of our popularity at the time, the band gradually drifted into midweek engagements and tours of Scotland lasting maybe six to eight weeks. This meant playing at venues nightly. My drinking pattern also changed from weekend to nightly. Tiredness probably played a large part in my urge for a drink.

I was now at the stage where I had a daily intake of alcohol. I was constantly topping myself up with just enough to see my performance through, though I would be counting the minutes until the last waltz arrived. This would be the cue for a really big bumper, straight out of the bottle. Unsuspectingly, I did not realise how dangerous this stage or progression was. When the bottle goes to your lips, you have lost the assessment (and safety net) of drink measurement. One gulp may very well equal three or four glasses of whisky.

In the 1960s and '70s, dances in village halls had no bar facilities.

Most people arrived with a half-bottle 'on the hip', as it was termed. Fergie was one of the boys, so a swig from a bottle was common practice. Ten swigs during a dance was no big deal. But my control of consumption by then was totally gone. By the end of the dance I would be over the limit, in other words drunk. Follow this with the usual 'after match' party, and by the early morning I would be horribly drunk. The cycle continues. You waken up after a few hours feeling really hellish, and the only cure is, of course, another dram. I didn't know it at the time, but I had graduated. I had joined the club, becoming a member of the fraternity of alcoholics. In my own case I was dependent on whisky.

I can truthfully say that the ten years from 1968 to 1978 were the worst years of my life. Just before moving from Glasgow to take up a senior physiotherapy post with the Highland Health Board in Fort William, I got married. Ann MacLeod, a beautiful and charming young lady of Skye and North Uist parentage, became my wife, and we were married by the Revd Angus MacKinnon in St Columba's Church, Glasgow.

Early in 1968 I had my first major alcohol-related catastrophe. I lost my driver's licence. One night, after playing at a dance in the Central Hotel, Glasgow, I was invited to a party with my accordion. In the early hours of the morning, blind drunk, I decided to go for a run out Great Western Road. What a stupid thing to do. At the Bowling roundabout my car crashed into an articulated lorry. In a drunken panic, my first reaction was to drive off. There were bits of my bumper and off-side front wing hanging off the car, not to mention a shattered windscreen. After being apprehended by the police, and charged at Clydebank Police Station, I was released and got a taxi back to my flat in Kelvinside.

Next day I had a feeling of remorse and utter humiliation to control. A brush with the police had been absolutely unheard of in my family. The conclusion of all this was a £200 fine and a one-year ban from driving. It seemed that the breathalyser recorded an extremely high reading of five times over the legal limit. The judge questioned my ability to stand up, far less drive. Today, I would probably have been jailed.

During this period of my life the 'Fergie MacDonald Band' were treated like pop stars. We were top of the tree on the Scottish ceilidh band scene. Then, suddenly, transport became a problem. Sometimes, when possible, Ann would drive me around to dance-band venues, but many of the engagements had to be cancelled, all at very short notice. I would be billed for, say, Campbeltown, and would have to cancel that very day due to my transport problem. These mounting difficulties became the excuse for severe bouts of drinking. This was in an effort to temporarily forget my mounting woes. It became a vicious circle.

At this stage I was, financially at least, pretty well-off. I had friends on every corner I turned. When heavy in on the drinking scene, with plenty of money, you are never without friends. Involvement with many women, in the form of one-night stands and secret relationships, seemed to go hand-in-hand with stardom and being in the public eye.

My capacity for alcohol seemed to become higher and higher. The down side of this was that longer periods of depression seemed to set in. Working at Gartnavel Psychiatric Hospital as a physiotherapist, one of my best friends was a young Indian doctor whom I used to party with. My pockets were always filled with as many tablets as I cared for. One tablet would take you from the depths of despair to an unbelievable high, while the next might have the opposite effect – from high to low. We discovered that mixing these drugs with strong beers or whisky produced amazing results. In short, here I was, away on another ball game: drugs and booze. All this was leading up to the 'big run-in', as described in alcoholic terms.

I decided to leave Glasgow and return north to Fort William, where my wife, Ann, drove me around my new physiotherapy practice, and to many dance venues. True to form, it is only a matter of time before an alcoholic surrounds himself and his family with severe domestic problems, often insurmountable. Music-wise, this meant short-notice cancellations, turning up drunk, appearing with half a band and not appearing at all. Soon it took its toll. The dance bookings dried up, and this led to financial crisis in the matrimonial home. Of course, every major row or confrontation led to even more consumption of alcohol. The endless circle continued. After a catalogue of walkouts and reconciliations, the situation became untenable, and separation, quickly followed by divorce, brought the marriage to an end.

Loneliness then comes into the equation. What kind of person really wishes to befriend a drunk? Consequences are that within an all too short period, the only friends that you have left are, bluntly, drinking buddies. Most of your friends and acquaintances have deserted and jumped ship. They don't want to know you any more. That is probably human nature.

The unthinkable continued: debt-collection officers, charges of assault and breach of the peace and, worst of all, health deterioration. That is tough, believe you me. Mind you, it is then, and only then, that real, true and genuine caring friends appear from nowhere. After spending a night in the police cells in Fort William for assault and drunkenness, and feeling utterly humiliated to say the least, the police inspector at the time, John MacInnes, an honest-to-goodness gentleman from the Isle of Skye, sent for me, and I was ushered up to his office. There was no lecture involved, only down to earth, fatherly advice. He got it over to me that my fall from grace had taken me from being an internationally known, respected member of the community, to 'down and out' status.

He said, 'Carry on down the road of self-destruction, and the next step, I can assure you Fergie, will be a stretch. No question about that.'

The word 'stretch' seemed to embed itself in my mind really firmly.

Eventually, in the law courts of Edinburgh, my marriage to Ann was dissolved 'decree nisi'. So there it was, the boy from Moidart who made it big time, was now back down the ladder on the very bottom rung. Life did not seem worth living, and suicide did cross my mind on a number of occasions.

That is what alcohol does to you. I felt so low and alone. When I consider it now, it was actually my attempts at sobriety which made me feel the worst. It is still alcohol which is behind it though. My own particular withdrawal symptoms brought on the most terrible bouts of depression. I would often question my very being. It seemed easier just to end everything there and then. I am sure that is a subject which crosses the mind of many an alcoholic at one time or another. I had decided that there wasn't an awful lot left for me on this earth, and that everyone would be better off without me. Looking back, it all seems so irrational, but then again, rationality is not something that the alcoholic is often familiar with.

It is a funny thing, but there is very little that I remember about the '70s. I have gone out of my way to blank them completely right out of my mind, because my alcoholism was so sad and tragic. As the decade wore on I eventually decided to come home to roost. I returned to the old croft house in Mingarry. But even at that, alcohol was still with me predominately. The regular routine on my way home from work was to call at Angus Peter MacLean's shop at Kinlochmoidart, and buy a half-bottle of whisky. This was a nightly occurrence. That, of course, was the fly one that was always kept outside, and would always be followed by a respectable two or three cans of beer in the house. Sometimes, you would even be enjoying a social dram at home, excusing yourself from the company every so often, with the usual excuse that you were going to the toilet. That was the cue for a right good glug out of your hidden store of booze. That is typically alcoholic procedure.

It all changed forever one night though. I can remember going through the usual routine. I stopped at Angus Peter's, but instead of buying my usual half-bottle, I went for a whole one. I remember it so well, a bottle of Whyte and MacKay. I jumped back in the car and made for home. I was coming over the hill at Kinlochmoidart, in view of Loch Shiel. That was always my halting place for a swig. I stopped the car, opened the bottle, and was in the process of raising it to my lips when I suddenly stopped dead. I looked at the bottle for long enough, read the label, where it had been made and all these things. I remember opening the driver's window and holding the bottle outside. I turned it upside down, emptied the lot, put the cork back on the bottle and threw it as far as I could. That was twenty-two years ago. That was my last dram!

I have, as I said, tried to forget the years wasted in the clutches of alcohol, but it is not easy. The painful memories have been slow to fade, and in all honesty are never far from my mind. Maybe that is a good thing. It is perhaps those very memories which have kept me 'on the wagon' for the past twenty-two years.

Having analysed my alcoholism, I can also see that there were some humorous moments too. This is not to make light of what is a very serious illness. On the contrary, I believe that it helps me come to terms with my situation; after all, it could be argued that there is a certain amount of humour in every human tragedy. In my experience, every alcoholic has some kind of fetish or leaning which tends to become exaggerated as part of their alcoholism. My own particular kick was letter-writing. I must have written thousands of letters while hitting the bottle. They were usually written in the wee small hours of the morning. That was when I would become highly intoxicated, and my mind would become highly charged. My scribing would usually start about two o'clock in the morning and carry on until daylight.

My second wife, Maureen, would often rise early in the morning ready to prepare breakfasts at the hotel. As often as not, she would discover me sitting at the kitchen table writing letters, having been nowhere near my bed. There would be a pile of letters beside me, all packed away in their envelopes, with addresses clearly marked and neatly written. Maureen would always be entrusted with the job of posting my handiwork. Years later I discovered, thankfully, that she had binned them every time. I used to write all sorts of letters to all sorts of people, but the most popular were letters of protest. I would write to the local MP (who happened to be Russell Johnston at the time) and local councillors (Dr Michael Foxley was very much in my sights) demanding explanations for all kinds of things that they simply couldn't have known about. Fortunately, Maureen dumped most of these straight away. There were a couple though which caught the eye and were kept for posterity. The one that really takes the biscuit was that of twenty pages that I wrote to the Pope. It was really quite hilarious. Maureen has kept the letter for a very long time, and I was given the privilege only recently of reading it.

At that particular time, I was one of the directors of Shona Recordings, a small record label specialising in Gaelic music and song.

My co-directors were local businessman, Allan MacColl, the well-known band leader and showbiz impresario, John Carmichael and 'Highland superstar', Norman MacLean. I decided (independently of the others) that Shona Recordings needed a massive showcase event to raise our profile and boost our record sales. To that end, I penned my letter to Pope John Paul with a view to hiring the Vatican for our extravaganza. In the letter, I quoted the names of my fellow directors and asked his Holiness if he would act as *Fear an Taighe* for the ceilidh, suggesting that it might be fitting to start off proceedings with a blessing and a prayer before he introduced the artistes.

There was quite a list of artistes, as I recall. The line-up included: Donald Angie Matheson from Barvas, Ishobel MacAskill, Calum Kennedy, Bobby MacLeod, Iain MacLachlan, Donald Archie MacKinnon from Broadford and quite a few others. There were pipers too. My old friend Allan MacPherson was in there along with Pipe Major John D. Burgess. My plan was that when the ceilidh finished, his Holiness would thank all the performers and then the dance would start. Allan MacColl was to be in charge of the money. He would go round with a biscuit tin collecting money from all the people in the Vatican enjoying this wonderful ceilidh. I thanked the Pope in anticipation and awaited his response with eagerness. Needless to say, I never did receive his blessing and he never did receive my letter. It's probably just as well.

22
Mine Host

It is an amazing thing really, how an alcoholic decided to become an hotelier. It's like throwing petrol onto a fire. Life can take some funny twists though.

I had just got married for the second time. I had been very wary of this, but after a long, five-year romance with Maureen, I bucked up enough courage to take the plunge for a second time. I had decided to start a brand new life. We headed home to Mingarry, in Moidart, where I took up the final post of my thirty-year physiotherapy career as a community domiciliary physiotherapist in the West Highlands. I enjoyed the posting very much, and it certainly wasn't without a laugh or two.

In those days the health board supplied all their medical staff in outlying areas with Austin 'minis' to help us get around our patients, and I can recall a very funny episode involving my Health Board car.

One day I was out shooting hinds around the Christmas period, and I had a problem getting all the beasts home, since my own van would not start because of the very cold weather. I decided that I would take the Health Board mini with me instead. That would have been the perfect solution, were it not for the fact that my local area superintendent physiotherapist, a Mr Bryson, was very strict about what the Health Board mini could and couldn't be used for. It was not to be used for anything other than Health Board purposes. The car was soon christened 'Bryson's mini'.

Anyway, on the day in question I had shot three hinds, and managed to get them down to the side of the road for loading into the mini, which I duly did. However, on the way home, I noticed a wee note which had been left on my windscreen, asking me to call at a local farm to collect three more hinds. I could foresee problems immediately. The mini was going to be far too small. I eventually collected the three extra beasts, which left me with a grand total of six hinds in 'Bryson's mini'.

Who did I happen to meet on the road, but my dear friend Angus Peter MacLean, who stopped and very nearly fell over when he saw the load in the Health Board car. He recalls the story to this day. One of the hinds was sitting in the front passenger seat with a seat belt round it. One was in the boot of the mini (how on earth I managed that I will never know). Three were in the back seat and the last one was strapped over the bonnet. Angus Peter could not believe what he was seeing, and his mental state was not helped by further inspection, which revealed the interior of the car to be floating in blood.

After leaving Angus Peter to recover from the shock, I proceeded home, where my wife Maureen was waiting for me with the news that 'Bryson' had been on the phone to tell me that my mini was needed the very next day by one of the district nurses over in Morvern. I was to be given another car which I was to collect in Fort William.

I left first thing the next morning to deliver the car (which poor Maureen had been up all night cleaning) to its new custodian in Morvern. I left it at the district nurse's house with a note which read 'from Fergie', along with instructions from Highland health board. This resulted in a fearful investigation altogether, because the nurse couldn't go anywhere near the car, with all the hair and patches of blood, not to mention the awful smell. She thought something terrible had happened in it, and she refused to use this Health Board mini that had come from Fergie. The end of it was that I was severely reprimanded over the mess that 'Bryson's mini' ended up in. That was a very serious incident at the time, but it's very funny when I think about it now.

I fell foul of the Health Board quite seriously on another occasion. I had to go and see a young female patient who had a biceps problem. The exercises which I had decided to give her involved flexion and extension of the arm, with a two-pound weight. The only problem was that I didn't have any weights with me. One gets used to improvising when travelling in rural areas, so I began looking around her house for something suitable, eventually finding an unopened tin of white 'high gloss' emulsion paint. I decide that this would be fine, as it was roughly two pounds in weight, so I showed her what to do and handed her the tin. Well, on the first extension of her arm, the 'high gloss' paint took off and landed on the brand new settee, spreading itself all over the three-inch-thick carpet. The place was covered.

That little incident cost the Health Board £5,000, and resulted in me being officially cautioned, for the one and only time in my career. I was told in no uncertain terms that if there were any more expenses incurred by Highland Health Board on my behalf, they would have no other option but to terminate my employment. Poor Mr Bryson, he never had it easy with me.

The funny thing was that although the carpet and settee were worth £5,000 at one time, a few of us suspected that the new owner had picked them up at a local 'bring and buy' sale for a fraction of that price.

I used to travel up to Glenelg quite often, as it fell under my jurisdiction, and it was there that I befriended a wonderful man called 'Gaffy' MacAskill, a retired policeman. He was suffering from a knee condition, and was referred to me by his local doctor. I have to say that my weekly run up to Glenelg was always a treat because of him. His knee was cured within six weeks (he received intensive treatment), and at that point should have been discharged from my list. 'Gaffy' had other ideas though, and wouldn't allow me to do this. He played the pipes and the fiddle, and loved it when I would bring the box in to have a tune with him. He loved it so much, in fact, that his treatment continued for three years.

His knee would mysteriously worsen every few weeks, and he would demand another referral. So I would turn up at the house again, and Mrs MacAskill would have the tea and sandwiches ready, knowing that I would be a while playing tunes with 'Gaffy'. I learned many, many tunes from him as well.

The button box eventually became part of my equipment. I took it everywhere on my rounds, and I honestly believe that it was a lot more therapeutic for many of my patients than more orthodox methods of physiotherapy.

There was a doctor once in Ardnamurchan called Dr Masson. He met me on the road one day and happened to look in the back of my Health Board car. There was a heat lamp, a short-wave diathermy unit, an accordion and a shot-gun.

'Fergie,' he said, 'you've got the right idea. If you can't cure them, you've got the means there to end all their pain and discomfort.'

I was enjoying my physiotherapy very much, as it was allowing me far more time at home, and my wife Maureen and I decided to look into the possibility of opening our own small family-run hotel. This would have been unthinkable before, but my move back to Moidart had facilitated the idea. My father and mother had Mingarry cottage as a croft house, but when we moved home, they moved into a chalet beside the house, and it was then that Maureen and I decided to make our move into the tourist industry.

We got planning permission and built rooms and a restaurant onto the family croft house. Then we applied for a table licence, which at first was met by a lot of local opposition. We eventually got the licence, and things ran fine for a year or two.

I decided at an early stage that music would be playing a large part in our new business, given its popularity with holidaymakers. To that end, we decided to build a bar. 'Fergie's Bar' it was known as. Again, after much local opposition and petitioning, it was decided that this would be of benefit to the whole area, which it certainly was. It opened up a brand new ball-game in the area, where music was very much to the fore. I was in the very fortunate position of being able to bring in top-line artistes. In fact, the local people (God bless them) were gifted with top-name performers, whom they had only ever dreamt of seeing. This probably bred complacency in the end. It became the norm that big, major stars would be appearing. That was what we were left with. Sub-standard artistes were no longer kindly accepted. They were looking for the Alexander Brothers and Andy Stewart and all these folk. Anyway, God bless them all. We were well supported by the majority of local people.

The most amazing thing was that the hotel business, which was absolutely foreign to me, opened up my eyes. It was actually Maureen who was running it. I was still involved as regional physiotherapy community officer for West Lochaber. While I was doing my rounds, attending to patients all day, Maureen was running the hotel. At nights I would join in, making music and helping to raise our family, Angela, John and Morven Ann, who were just children then.

That was quite a difficult period for them. They, as young children, were at an age when, try as you might to control them, they would jump out of bed at eleven o'clock at night, looking for Mum and Dad, and arrive over in the bar and start screaming. People would start walking out. I suppose that was part of the whole jigsaw.

The hotel life is a world all of its own though. I hadn't long given up the booze, and what I found most difficult was making small talk with people in the bar. It suddenly became one big bore to me. We had to get bar staff in because I just couldn't hack it. It is amazing an alcoholic not being able to work in a bar. It brought it home to me, the realisation that people must have been bored with the nonsense I talked when I was on the drink.

There have been many amazing incidents. I remember one night that these two men arrived. They were booked into room three. The hotel was full and we were living in a caravan next door. In the middle of the night, a woman who was staying in the hotel came and knocked on our door. She said, 'You'll have to come out Mr MacDonald, and put a stop to this amazing noise that's coming out of room three.'

I went over to the hotel, and I can honestly say that I had never heard a noise like that in my life; groans and grunts. It seemed as if they were belting each other senseless. You would hear screaming, and furniture going flying. The noise was incredible. Every guest in the hotel was downstairs listening to this upheaval.

It was my job to go and stop all this nonsense, so I knocked on the door and shouted in at them. They both came out at once. There they were. One of them had boxing gloves on. He was hammering hell out of this other poor soul. The other one had no clothes on at all, except for knickers, stockings and suspenders, with this other guy skelping the hell out of him. These kinds of incidents really do open your eyes.

Another time, there was a French car parked at the side of the hotel. It was lunchtime, and we were expecting a Shearings coach to arrive. We were busy readying ourselves, and paid no attention to the fact that two people had come out of the car and used the loos. That was fine. In fact, it was quite a regular occurrence. The bus soon arrived, and of course, the first thing people do when they come of a coach is go to the loo, poor souls. One woman came out almost immediately, and asked to see the management. I explained that I was the manager. She said, 'Would you please take a look in the ladies' toilet? We are definitely not eating on your premises.' I asked why. Then another lady came over and said, 'We have never experienced anything like this in our lives!' I decided that I had better take a look. I went into the lavatory, and I can honestly say that the floor, ceiling and the walls were covered in shit. I had never seen anything like it.

Whoever had been in had used their hands to decorate the whole of the loo with the stuff. It was the most revolting scene. It makes you wonder what homes folk come from. The maids who were working in the hotel wouldn't go near it, so it was left to Maureen to get a brush and bucket and get stuck right into it. That really makes you wonder what the other half are like.

The continentals are amazing. There was once a Frenchman arrived at the hotel. Pierre was his name; I remember it fine. He was a hunter. He had come to shoot stags. He would have been about fifty years old, and was accompanied by this beautiful young 'bird', with long red fingernails. She was a real dolly bird. Prior to his arrival, all communication had been with his office, in Bordeaux. The only contact address and phone number that we had was for his office.

Eventually this couple landed at Glasgow Airport, and took a taxi all the way up to Moidart. They were staying in one of the chalets at the hotel for a week. He went out shooting every day, and I remember that he always took this length of beautiful silk rope with him. We were crossing a burn one day, and Angus Peter MacLean, who was with us, wondered how we were going to get the dead stag across. The Frenchman went into his haversack and produced this wonderful rope, which we tied around the stag to haul it over the water.

The week came to an end, and Pierre and the young lady left in the early hours of Saturday morning to catch their flight from Glasgow. Once again a taxi had been booked, which took them all the way south. Janet Stewart, a local woman who was working with us, had been detailed to clean out the chalet for the next customers, who were coming in that day. She came back with a bag that the Frenchman had left. I told Janet to leave the bag with me, and that I would phone the man the next day at his office. The next morning I was straight onto the phone.

'Hello Pierre,' I said. 'You have left a bag with us.'

'Oh yes, I was just going to phone you about that,' he said.

'That's alright,' I said. 'I'll just parcel it up and send it home if you give me your address.'

Pierre nearly hit the roof. 'No! You must not send it to my home address!'

I wondered why not, but he would not tell me, giving me a completely different address altogether. I was certainly intrigued by his panic, so, as we were packing the bag up, we decided to have a quick look inside. I have never seen a bag like it in my life. There were handcuffs, face masks, suspenders, love toys, jellies, ropes – the lot. And here was me going to send it to his home address! I can just imagine what would have happened had I sent it there. His wife would have loved that.

These are the sort of folk that you find yourself up against in the hotel game. Having said that, you do meet many wonderful people; but there is always the occasional weirdo. That's life of course. You just have to get on with it.

We leased the hotel out for a while to a nice young couple from Uist, but they moved on to bigger and better things, and now the Clanranald is run by my daughters, Angela and Morven. They seem to like the life. They haven't met any outrageous people yet, although I am sure it is not too far in the distance. I have thoroughly enjoyed my life in the hotel business, though I don't have much to do with it now. I just go over occasionally and play a tune for the guests on my accordion.

23
Clay Pigeons

When I was a boy in Acharacle, there was a clay-pigeon shoot held every Christmas Day at Shiel Bridge. When I was very, very young, I used to hear the noise of the guns being fired, as it was only a mile from our family home. You would hear constant gunfire for hours on end.

Being brought up in a sporting home, full of guns and rifles, my father took me over to see the shooting match one Christmas. I don't suppose I was all that old, but I liked very much what I saw and, at the end of the shoot, my father asked Ronnie MacMaster, one of the local gamekeepers, if he would give me a shot. Ronnie, being the gentleman that he was, took me in hand, stood behind me, showed me where to point the gun (I could hardly hold it) and shouted 'pull'. A black pigeon came flying out of the trap and I let fly at it, smashing it into smithereens. I don't know whether that was an omen or not, but I was over the moon. As it happens, I missed the next five. That is often the way it works out.

At the same shoot, the following year, Ronnie MacMaster entered me as a competitor for the day's shooting, using his shotgun, with him standing behind me. This was to become an annual event, and I competed every year until I left to do my national service. It was a great day out and great fun. There was always a wonderful article match at this shoot, with haunches of venison and a cup as prizes, and a shield for the team shoot. It was a wonderful occasion. Everyone would be having a dram behind the organiser's tent, until it would reach the stage where nobody could hit a bird at all.

The annual shoot was something that I thoroughly enjoyed,

although it would be wrong to suggest that clay pigeon shooting had become a major part of my life. However, due to unforeseen circumstances in the years ahead, it eventually would.

As time went by, and I became involved in music and entertainment, I was led into the world of social, habitual and ultimately compulsive drinking. In short, I became an alcoholic. As you know, I have fought a battle with this chronic illness for many years now, and although one can never say that one is fully cured, I have managed to free myself from the jaws of alcoholism.

When that happens you suddenly find that you have hours of free time on your hands. In fact, you could very easily revert to the bottle. Kicking the habit requires a major transformation in your life. When you are drinking heavily you lose days and weeks that you simply cannot account for. Suddenly, here I was with all this spare time on my hands, so I decided that something must be done about it.

I bought a *Shooting Times* one day, which had a list of all the shooting matches taking place all over Scotland. I began to think that taking up shooting as a hobby might not be a bad idea, so I bought myself a five-shot Remmington twelve-bore shotgun, and began competing at local matches. I began to get more and more hooked the more I competed, and it developed into what one might call an obsession. I got very interested in the whole world of shooting, looked into the whole thing, and became very good at it.

It wasn't long before I began to think about selection matches for the Scottish international team, ten of which take place every year. They are staged all over the country, from Wick and Thurso to Loch Ness and Ayrshire, and one has to submit one's five best scores. It was very difficult getting your scores. You were up against such brilliant opposition as the Carsons from Dalbeattie, Louis Stewart from Inverness, Mark Campbell from Thurso – all amazing shooters. It also meant a lot of travelling to various shoots all over Scotland, although we used to have wonderful fun in the process. There were so many funny incidents at the qualifying matches that it would take another book to record them all.

One that springs to mind happened at a large hundred-bird shoot at Dalmellington, in Ayrshire. My three shooting friends, the MacColl brothers, Charlie and Ewen, and Angus MacDonald, an ex-policeman from North Uist, had asked me to book accommodation for us all for the weekend. So I did my best. I booked us into this most amazing place that I had found through the Ayrshire tourist board. Bed and breakfast was £4 each. That in itself gives you some idea as to the standard of the accommodation that awaited us. Angus MacDonald's television was on top of the wardrobe. When he went to switch it on, the whole wardrobe collapsed and the television ended up on his bed. Charlie, Ewen and Angus weren't really all that happy with the digs I had found for them.

At the same shoot, I was having awful problems with a rash on my groin, which I told the boys about. I explained that I would need to get powder for it.

'Och, that's alright,' said Angus, 'I'll nip down to the chemist and find something for you.'

I thought this was very good of him, never once questioning his motives. He arrived back shortly and handed me this tin of powder, which he told me to slap on. This I duly did, liberally covering my groin area and private parts in the stuff. I ended up in agony all night long, while the other three rolled about laughing in their beds. After further investigation, I found out that the mystery potion that Angus had bought me was in fact 'scouring powder'. None of us managed a score of any consequence the next day. We were too busy laughing at Angus's miracle cure.

The first year I tried for selection I nearly made it, but not quite. However, the second year, I recorded five good scores and entered the world of international clay-pigeon shooting. I had been selected to shoot in the Scottish international team, and remained a part of the squad for twelve years, amassing fourteen international caps, of which I am very proud indeed.

I missed the local events terribly at first, but realised that I had the talent to move on. I can still remember the day when the penny finally dropped, at the Morvern shooting match, which was always held during the third week in May at Claggan. There were 105 competitors that day, with five trophies up for grabs; the 'aggregate', the 'ten bird', the 'fifteen bird', the 'five bird gun down' and the 'double rise'. I succeeded in winning all five competitions, which was quite an achievement, given the standard of shooter that I was up against. There were so many competitors that the match went on until after nine o'clock in the evening.

People began to take heed of me then. It was suggested that I should be looking at 'hundred bird' matches and possible selection for the Scottish team. For better or worse, that is exactly what I did, although shooting never did hold the same fascination for me after that. It was also very tough. The way I look at it, if you take a four-cornered international between Scotland, Ireland, England and Wales, you are standing there, with your Scotland vest on, representing your country. This makes your first time out an extremely nerve-racking experience, as the standard is so incredibly high.

At international level, a match usually consists of shooting at 100 clay pigeons, in batches of twenty-five. You can forget about winning if you score less than ninety-eight or ninety-nine kills. You have to be in that bracket consistently to enjoy any success at that level and that takes a bit of doing, I can assure you!

My favourite international match was always shooting against the Irish in Dublin. We all know how Ireland is divided, with Ulster in the north and the Republic in the south. This does not count in shooting. The team is all-Ireland, the same as the rugby union side. That, in my book, breeds nothing but goodness. We had some great times shooting against Ireland. It was always the case that nobody really cared who won, as the *craic* was so good.

Shooting against England, on the other hand, was a different ball-game all together. You always wanted to win, although they were always very difficult to beat. To beat them is the biggest kick of all for being a patriotic Scotsman. Though during my involvement with the national team we only beat them once, which is a pretty bad record. Mind you, it seems to be like that in every sport that we play against them.

I shot my last international match in Wales in 1994. I was just beginning to go downhill then, for to shoot at that level your eyesight and reflexes must be in the plus-plus category. These talents were just starting to go at that time. I remember the last shoot well though, as

I ended up with 100 kills, and that made me happy. I went out in the way that I wanted – at the top.

I haven't shot since that day, for once you are out, you are out. I have never gone back to shooting at small local events, and I am sure that is my Highland pride coming out in me. You see, if an internationalist goes to a local shoot, everyone wants to beat him. When you get older and past it, you will get beaten by pretty mediocre marksmen, and to put it bluntly I don't want to give anyone that satisfaction. I would rather have met them thirty years ago, and shown them what it was all about. That's only my way of looking at it. Maybe I've got it wrong, but I don't shoot anymore.

Of course I still miss the social aspect of clay-pigeon shooting. It wasn't always deadly serious competition. The local shoots were often magical occasions, with fun being the operative word. All the local gamekeepers would turn out, Allan MacColl and Ronnie MacMaster, whom I mentioned previously, and many of the fine local marksmen, like Iain and Duncan Smith, Alasdair Grey, Iain MacColl, Tommy Ross, Ronnie MacLeod, George Nairn and so many other good shooters, thoroughly enjoying themselves at a local shoot in Blaich, Glenfinnan, Morvern, Black Mount, Kilchoan or any of the other local matches. It never really mattered all that much who won or lost. It was always more important that you were spending a day enjoying each other's company.

Later, when I graduated into the international field, the sport lost much of its lustre. All the fun went out the window. It was a question of winning at all costs. That was in stark contrast to the local events, in which my love for the sport was first born.

I was once involved in an awful escapade at a shooting match in Tobermory, on the island of Mull. Such was the revelry that many of the boys (myself included) from Moidart, Morvern and Ardnamurchan missed the ferry home. Luckily, our shooting friends on Mull were able to put us up for the night. We were billeted out with the likes of Alasdair MacLean, big Iain Morrison and Johnny MacDonald in Dervaig. This, of course, signalled the start of an almighty drinking session.

We had a most wonderful night in Tobermory. When the shooting match was over (I haven't a clue what the result was) we all met back at the Mishnish Hotel, which was run and owned by my old friend Bobby MacLeod. Closing time in the 'Mish' heralded a mass exodus to a party in Dervaig, where we stayed for some time before returning in the early hours to Tobermory. That, however, was far from the end of our night.

We ended up on a fishing boat which was berthed in the harbour (I can't give you the name or I would get the jail). It was decided that this would be the perfect venue for a continuation of the festivities. Things were continuing apace, until it was decided to hold a competition to see who had the biggest manhood. A young English woman, who had strayed into no-man's-land, was handed a ruler and given the job of measuring the competitors. I was the one left with the notepad and pencil, taking down vital statistics to the last sixteenth of an inch. It was obviously important that we got it right, because there was a bottle of whisky at stake. Fortunately, or unfortunately, depending on your view, the competition was abandoned halfway through, when the wife of the vessel's owner (himself a competitor and looking good for a medal) made a most unwelcome appearance below decks. She chased us all off the boat, calling us a disgrace to clay-pigeon shooting, and her poor husband was banned from shooting for the next year. What a finale! We never did find out who was the champion!

24
My Father

There has been a long history of fine marksmen in my family, and I am happy to say that the tradition has been passed on to my son. There have been few better crack shots in the clan than my own father, John, who was born in 1892, the eldest of nine children. He came from a long line of gamekeepers. Fishing and shooting were his life. As a young man (round about 1910) he joined the newly-formed local territorial-army battalion of the Lovat Scouts, whose captain was Lord Howard, the local estate owner at the time. His timing was unfortunate, as when the Great War began in 1914, he was amongst the first of the troops to be called up.

They were based first of all down in Norfolk, during 1914. They were training with horses (as they were a cavalry regiment) around the Wash area, when all of a sudden the horses were taken away from them. They were suddenly turned into infantry, with no warning or proper training whatsoever. The Lovat Scouts, the Scottish Horse, the Fife and Forfars, the Yorkshire Yeomanry; all these cavalry regiments suddenly found themselves without horses. It was decided that they would head out to the Dardanelles, to fight the Turks as infantry, and that is exactly what happened.

The Lovat Scouts were soon dispatched, and landed in Suvla Bay in August 1915. They remained in the Dardanelles until their eventual evacuation. It was all trench warfare. I heard so many stories about this time, and they are embedded in my mind because I heard them so often.

One morning, in the middle of winter, a heavy snowfall which had covered the ground for several weeks began to thaw, and the trenches (both British and Turkish) began to fill up with water. I will always remember my father telling me of how the Turks were eventually compelled to abandon their trenches. My father was in a section very close to the Turkish lines as they began to evacuate into no-man's-land. They had to, or they would have drowned. Such is the horror of war that the order was given to open fire. No quarter was to be given. A friend of my father's, who was also present, once told me that it was like a morning shooting hinds. Anyone who has seen a hillside in winter, red with the blood of deer, will know what he meant. It must have been horrific.

Such events were often followed by long periods of inactivity. During these times, loneliness and boredom were one's biggest enemies. Many of the young lads from Moidart were stationed together, in a trench close to the Turkish lines, and they used to play a dangerous game to keep themselves on their toes.

There was a sniper on the Turkish side whom they had nicknamed 'Perse'. He was a crack shot who had accounted for countless numbers of British troops. Every day, the boys would take a shovel and wave it above the parapet of the trench. If Perse was not on duty, nothing would ever happen, but if he was, there would be a bullet hole through the blade of the shovel within seconds. That was the calibre of the opposition they faced.

One day an order came through from the divisional HQ. Perse was to be dealt with. He had claimed too many lives, and the 'top brass' decided that he would have to be taken dead or alive. The location of his dugout was soon confirmed through skilful reconnaissance, and a detachment of troops (roughly company strength) was sent over in the middle of the night to put an end to his deadly work.

The troops surprised Perse, and it was a young soldier from Sutherland who fired the fatal shot. The young soldier was himself wounded badly during the attack, as another Turk managed to bayonet him as he pulled the trigger. My father could remember him being taken back along the British trench on a stretcher, which had Perse's rifle strapped to it. Luckily, the young soldier from Sutherland survived his wounds and the rest of the war. Perse's rifle would most certainly have been taken home to Sutherland, and hopefully is still in the possession of someone who realises its significance and knows the story behind it. Incidentally, when Perse was killed, he was found to be wearing somewhere in the region of a hundred British dog tags on a string around his neck.

As a sniper, my father must have had many registered kills himself, and would often have seen his victim at close quarters. He never talked about this though. I never even remember him so much as broaching the subject at any time. It was something which he kept locked inside all his life. I certainly never asked him how many men he had killed, but I remember, as a youngster, without knowing what they were, I used to play with little tags, which my father had taken home from the war himself. In later life I learned that British snipers played the same game as the Turks, which involved collecting as many identification tags as they could from enemy soldiers that they had shot. My father's tags actually came from German soldiers killed on the Western Front. What a horrible, bloody game! I would be guessing as to how many he had in a box, but there were an awful lot.

My father was himself almost the victim of a sniper's bullet. He was a battalion sniper at the time and had been detailed to carry out a night-time reconnaissance in no-man's-land, as part of a four-man team. Before leaving, he had been in his dugout getting his kit ready and couldn't find his belt. He had a friend from Moidart with him, Donald MacDonald (Dòmhall Mhìchael), and he asked him if he could borrow his. Donald handed him his belt and my father went off as part of the four-man team.

On returning the next morning, my father found Donald MacDonald, and threw him the remains of his belt. He thanked Donald and told him that it had saved his life. During the night, my father had been hit by a bullet, which struck the belt buckle, smashing it to pieces, but protecting my father from any injury. You don't get many closer calls than that. Incidentally, that belt was taken home and was lying in Donald's sister's house for years and years until her death. My father expressed an interest in acquiring the belt as a souvenir, but he was too late, as Donald's relatives had cleared out the house, and thrown the belt on the fire, believing it to be an old razor strop.

After their eventual evacuation from the Dardanelles, the Lovat

Scouts returned to Britain for a brief period of rest. It was during this period of rest that my father heard of a special detachment which was to be raised within the regiment. The detachment was to consist of eight groups of snipers and reconnaissance troops, who would eventually be used to fight a new style of warfare against the Germans in France. Members would be hand picked, and had to prove themselves better than their fellow soldiers in terms of fitness, fortitude, resourcefulness and bravery. Above all else, they would have to be marksmen of the highest order. Nothing else would do. They were to be known as the 'Lovat Scouts Sharp Shooters'.

My father passed selection and was sent to Beaufort Castle near Beauly (the family home of the regiment's colonel, Lord Lovat), for special training. After training, they were sent to France, and the Somme, where they would eventually face the enemy in one of the bloodiest battles in the history of human conflict.

Each group had about thirty snipers in it, and my father was stationed with number eight group. The commanding officer of my father's group was Captain John MacGillivray, who was a great-uncle of the world-renowned piper, Duncan MacGillivray. They were a close-knit bunch, who operated unlike any other part of the army at that time. They referred to each other using Christian names, and although respect was given for ranks, they were never used when addressing officers. It was very much like the modern-day SAS. In fact, in later life, my father was presented with a plaque from Lord Lovat which bore the famous winged dagger of the Special Air Service.

Whilst in France, they operated in two-man teams. My father's second man was a young gamekeeper from Glen Affric by the name of Willie Boa. They arrived on the Somme in early 1917, and had no leave whatsoever until May 1918. They were fourteen months under almost constant shellfire. Number eight group of the sharp shooters were based around the Cambrai area. I can still remember the names, 'Mount Saint Quentin', 'Bapaume'.

The stories from this period of my father's life were incredible. Where does one begin? After all, I heard so many.

One of the best lessons my father ever taught me about stalking was related to his own near fatal experience during the final German offensive of 21 March 1918. The offensive opened up, as usual, with an artillery barrage, which lasted about four hours. My father and Willie Boa were out of the line during this initial action. They found themselves thirty feet down in a bunker, with a lamp which refused to stay lit because of the bombardment. When the barrage abated, the Sharp Shooters were detailed to keep an eye on frontline German movements and report back to headquarters. Each two-man team was given a different sector to reconnoitre.

My father and Willie Boa were given the task of monitoring German movements across a river in the local vicinity. The two of them were perched above the river on the Allied side, and were watching all the activity on the other bank, as the Germans prepared to cross. My father was watching them through his spy glass, constructing pontoon bridges, when Willie Boa happened to look down towards their left flank. Their own side of the river was crawling with Germans who had managed to get across. Obviously, concentrating on the activity directly opposite, the two of them had missed an area where the Germans were already able to cross.

Willie Boa kicked my father's backside as hard as he could, shouting 'Get the hell out of here John!' They grabbed what they could and fled, as the Germans (thousands of them) were only metres away. They ran and ran and ran, until they reached safety.

My father always taught me afterwards, that when you are stalking, you always start spying right beside you and work out the way. It was a lesson which almost cost him his life. That episode also saw the two of them nearly break another golden rule, which was that sharp shooters were never to be caught. This rule was drummed into them from the start, and was established because of pamphlets which the Germans had dropped over Allied lines. These showed a picture of a Lovat Scouts sharp shooter, and listed all the things that the Germans would do to them, if they ever caught one of them. That was enough of an incentive never to get caught.

They had been operating on the Somme front for a year before that particular offensive. Most of their time had been spent in no-man's-land, which is where all the action happened for the snipers. They always wore their famous Lovat Scouts' 'Balmoral' with its distinctive green colouring and green and white check round the brim. They would wear a camouflage veil over this while out on operations. It was very important, as a sniper, that no part of your uniform or equipment was visible, or glinted in sunlight, as this was always a giveaway of your position, and would mean almost certain death. They were also warned of the dangers of firing at a target more than once, as a second shot would often pinpoint the sniper's location. 'One shot, one kill' was the unwritten rule of the sharp shooters.

On one particular occasion my father and Willie Boa were preparing to go out to a hide in no-man's-land, when who appeared back but the two boys they were being sent to relieve. One of them was John MacHardy from Inverie in Knoydart. His Balmoral had been shot clean off. The pathway of the bullet was right through the top of his hat. The dicing or check on his hat had been spotted by a sharp-eyed German and had given the hide away.

Some of my father's stories from this period also had a humorous side. Captain MacGillivray used to receive a case of whisky once a month from a distillery in Speyside. This was for the purpose of cleaning the lenses on the sniper's rifle, his telescope and his binoculars. Needless to say, very few of the twelve bottles ever went near a lens, but were put to good use for all that. There was always a party on the night when the bottles arrived, with everyone available invited to join in. This indiscretion was always overlooked by the officers, given the conditions that the men were fighting under.

On another occasion, my father found himself on the run for over a month, during the final big German offensive. The British line had been breached, and the order was given to retreat. It was a case of 'every man for himself'. My father and Willie Boa found themselves in a group of six sharp shooters while on the run. One of them was a strong, strong man from Kintail, called Finlay MacRae. He emigrated to Detroit after the war, and wrote to my father for years, in a bid to convince him that his future lay across the Atlantic too.

While retreating, they reached a French village, and discovered a wine cellar below the local café. They smashed into it with the butts of their rifles, and found an underground room stocked high with booze. They loaded bottles upon bottles of wine into their haversacks, before getting stuck into their cargo in some quiet spot. On leaving the village, they joined a long line of soldiers and refugees, all fleeing from the vicinity, when they were suddenly set upon by German planes, who strafed them all with machine-gun fire. Rows and rows of people threw themselves into ditches in an attempt to save their lives. You could see the bullets digging up the road as people dived for cover. Luckily everyone made it to safety. Everyone, that is, apart from Finlay MacRae, who was lying on his belly in the middle of the road, sniper's rifle above his head, blasting away at the planes. My father said that poor Finlay, like the rest of them, was blind drunk. It is a miracle that he wasn't killed.

By the grace of God, my father too was spared and survived the war, though it definitely left its mark on him. I'll always remember him as one of the kindest people I've ever known, and generous to a fault. He thought so much of his family, and would have done anything for us. But I could see, as I got older, that the terrible carnage of the Somme had left its indelible mark.

Sometimes my mother would be terrified, as my father would wake up screaming and shouting in the middle of the night. Obviously he had returned to the war in his sleep. His cries would be terrible. He must have been only one of countless thousands forever haunted by the senseless waste of war. I hope and pray that future generations never have to go through the same ordeal.

My father never held any animosity towards the German people. He rated them very highly, and I often remember him describing them as 'decent, ordinary people'. He had no hate in his heart for them at all, at all. In fact, he admired them all his life. What he often said was that the Germans were brave soldiers, doing exactly the same as he was doing, but it is clear that this respect was not always shared by his comrades.

I remember him telling me about a chap called Urquhart who served alongside him in France. He was reckoned to be a top-notch sniper, but pretty callous with it. In short, he was a nasty piece of work. One day they were watching a long line of German prisoners being taken by, when Urquhart suddenly walked into the line and stopped one of them. He had noticed a ring that the German was wearing and fancied it for himself, so he began pulling at it but couldn't remove it. After a few attempts he turned to my father and shouted, 'Give me your knife John.' Daddy wasn't amused at this at all, at all, at all, and I think he flattened Urquhart there and then.

My father especially admired the German snipers, believing them to be brilliant. He often said that you couldn't show them your thumb without it getting blown off. They were of the highest calibre as far as he was concerned, and that seemed to excite him. I've often felt that despite the horror, part of him viewed the war as a game. A deadly game, but a game never the less.

On returning to Moidart, he worked as the local postman for many years. Sometimes this would involve rowing over to Eilean Shona with the mails, on other occasions, a five-mile walk to Gortenfern. On one of these sorties, during the Second World War, my father had to walk through a mock battle which had been set up by the commandoes. The officer in charge of the exercise was suddenly perplexed to see this figure making his way through the middle of the training area, shells and mortars exploding all around his chosen path. His perplexity was possibly increased by the fact that special forces always trained with live ammunition; a fact which everyone in the area, including my father, knew fine well.

The officer commanding stopped the battle, demanding to know just who this maniac was. He was soon told that it was the local postman, on his way from Arivegaig to Gortenfern. A junior officer was hastily dispatched to warn my father of the danger, and on approaching him, asked in a rather irritated tone, 'Do you know there's a battle going on?'

My father stared at the young officer and said, 'A battle?' He shook his head and carried on his way.

It was only afterwards that the young officer was informed of my father's exemplary war record and his experiences under fire.

He lived a long life and remained active well into his nineties. I remember him sitting outside the hotel one summer's night. He would have been ninety at the time. He was watching half a dozen local boys (some of whom were internationals) shooting clay pigeons. One of the shooters, James MacLellan, had acquired a .22 BSA rifle with open sights, and was busy showing it to the other boys. For a bit of sport, a matchstick was stuck on top of a fence post at a range of thirty yards, and everyone was invited to have a shot at hitting it. We went through round after round of ammunition. All these international crack shots had a go at it. I even had a go at it myself, but nobody got near it. Eventually, somebody turned to my father and said, 'Here John, you have go.' At first he declined, but after watching a few more attempts he decided to have a try. He was passed the loaded rifle, and continued to sit in his chair, as he raised it to his shoulder. Without any support whatsoever, he took aim and fired. None of us had ever seen anything like it. He not only hit the match, but lit it in the process. Everyone stood in stunned silence. He was asked to try it again, but was fly enough to repeat the sharp shooter's mantra: 'One shot, one kill!' He had been trained never to fire more than once.

25
Religious Beliefs

In my early life, I was brought up a Roman Catholic. In those days, Roman Catholicism had a very strict code of conduct. The school, in Mingarry, was a Catholic one where the catechism and every aspect of Catholic life were hammered home. There is no other way of putting it. It was a one-way ticket. If you weren't a Catholic, you were doomed. From there, you graduated to being an altar boy in our beautiful little church, 'Our Lady of the Angels'. That was the religion I was born into.

The interesting thing was that my father was of Catholic origin, going back as far as we can trace our forefathers in Moidart, but my mother was Free Presbyterian. She was from Morvern, being able to trace her family line directly back to the famous Gaelic bard, Dr John MacLachlan of Rahoy. In fact most of the male members of my mother's family, almost to a man, were doctors or ministers.

It is only now that I realise what an upheaval it must have been for my mother. I wonder how on earth she managed to wrench herself away from Presbyterianism and turn to Roman Catholicism. Having said that, as a child, I must have suffered from some sort of religious schizophrenia. She never lost her Presbyterian background or outlook. She still practised it daily. My mother never said the Lord's Prayer in the manner of the Catholic Church, and I certainly wasn't allowed to play or make music on a Sunday. The radio was certainly banned on the Lord's Day, as were cutting logs, making hay, fishing or shooting. All these things were totally banned. It was simply taboo. That was my early life on the one hand; but on the other side I had the Catholic thing biting in.

I reached an age where I took stock of myself, and in all honesty I didn't know what I was. That state of mind saw me through my army years, and slowly, but surely, I drifted away from all forms of organised religion and church-going. I drifted right through my student days in the same way. Religion never came into it. Maybe that is because I didn't know what my true identity was. Half my family were Free Presbyterian, the other half Roman Catholic. In the Highlands, there is no question that that is a major divide in every sense.

When I married for the first time it could have been anybody, but it so happened that it was Ann, although we nearly never did get married. In fact, the story I am about to relate nearly caused the cancellation of two weddings.

I had a great friend from Kinlochleven, Donald MacKenzie, who was a policeman in Dunbartonshire at the time. Donald was a keen box player, and the two of us used to meet up for a ceilidh now and again. He was due to get married the same week as me. Donald arrived at my flat on Great Western Road late one night, in full uniform, with a bottle of whisky under his arm. He had parked the squad car outside, and had decided to call in for a dram. We got talking, and it turned out that Donald was going on his marriage leave the very next day, so we got stuck into the whisky, and by three in the morning we were just blazing; playing our boxes and as happy as Larry. Tongues suddenly began to get looser, and ideas began to get bigger. We had a long serious chat, and decided that marriage was not for us. We were not going to go through with it. We discovered that the whole set-up was irretrievably flawed, and decided to bail out. I packed my bag (and my accordion) and at six o'clock in the morning we hit the trail. At seven o'clock, Donald signed off in Dumbarton, and we tore up the road in his car. We didn't care where we were going as long as it was in a northerly direction: the call of the hills. By eight o'clock we were playing our boxes at Loch Lomond side.

Suddenly Donald had a brainwave. He had a brother who was a gamekeeper in the 'Black Corries', Glencoe. He suggested that this would be the perfect place to hide until the heat died down. I agreed. It was in May, and there was a heat wave, so we had a wonderful time shooting and fishing, and drinking and playing our boxes.

We made one fatal mistake however. We took our accordions down every night to the King's House Hotel, where we would play for all the climbers and hill-walkers. We had great nights there, enjoying the management's hospitality, but soon word spread around the locality. The place ended up packed night after night. You would turn up around 8 p.m., and not leave until four in the morning. It wasn't long before word spread further afield that Donald MacKenzie and Fergie MacDonald were in King's House Hotel. After that, it was just a matter of time before we were caught.

We were both retrieved, under duress, and taken back to Glasgow, where we were forced to go through with our respective marriages. The thing was though, that both marriages ended after a short period of time, and I've often wondered if there was a wee warning somewhere along the line.

Anyway, what I was going to say was that I did marry Ann. She was not Catholic, and I had no hang-up about getting married 'outside the church', as it is known. This, however, did not go down well with my own local parish priest in Moidart. I was what is generally known in the business as 'excommunicated'. I have to say that excommunication never bothered me all that much. Then divorce came along, which did not bother the priest all that much, as I had been married outwith the Catholic Church.

There are so many different aspects involved in religion; so many, in fact, that nobody will ever sort out the differences. There are pluses and minuses for all religions.

The second time I married was also outwith the Catholic Church, which again posed no problem. It is an amazing thing though, the old conscience. Your childhood and upbringing slowly begin to start working on you. I decided that after all, I felt a drawing back towards Catholicism. With the help of Cannon Joseph Terry, a gentleman of the highest degree, I returned. He managed to get me, for want of a better word, reinstated. And much to the credit of my wife, Maureen, we had our marriage blessed in a private ceremony, involving close family and friends, in our little church in Mingarry.

I was accepted back into the flock with open arms, and I was very happy for once in my life. I began to practise my religion again, though not heavily it has to be said. I have never been heavy on it, but at least I was going to church and receiving the sacraments with my family. This was not to continue though. I have often wondered if my fellow Catholics held it against me, all those years when I deserted them. I wondered if I was viewed as a deserter back in the ranks. I began to find things very awkward. Indeed, things got so awkward that I felt I was being ganged up on. A certain sect of my fellow Catholics, along with the priest, more or less banished me for a second time from the Church, through their awkwardness and bloody-mindedness. I can only hope and pray that, if God gives me the chance, one day I will be allowed to die in the faith in which I was brought up.

26
Rebirth

As you now know, I managed to break free of the clutches of alcohol round about the 1980 mark. It is amazing just how much it affects you. Total blame for my tragic downfall was, in my eyes, to be laid squarely at the door of my involvement with music. I blamed the whole music scene, and the circles of friends one tends to mix in as a result of such an involvement, for my ruin. How wrong I was. Basically, I was the problem. Music was not to blame for my alcoholism, though it took me a long time to realise it.

My immediate reaction was to pack my accordion away, seldom playing it, if ever. I would manage the odd function and maybe a tune in the house. I had convinced myself that music was the foe. This meant that my accordion-playing took a back seat for many, many years. I was not to know it, but my musical rebirth would only begin after a chance meeting in the hotel one day.

It was the late 1980s, and on the particular day in question I was busy in the hotel, when a young gentleman walked in. We got speaking, and he told me that his name was Phil Cunningham and that he had wanted to meet me for a long time. The name meant nothing to me, because when you are out of the game like that, you lock yourself away; you lose touch. You do not know who's who, or what musicians or bands are top-line anymore.

He looked up at the wall, where I had many of my albums displayed, and he told me that he had nearly every one in his house. I was quite taken by this and asked him if he liked music, or whether he played a wee bit himself. He informed me that he did, and that he could rattle out a tune or two on the box.

'One of the things I would love,' he said, 'is to play a tune with you. I've been playing your records since I was a youngster.'

I was only too happy to oblige, and told him to go and get his accordion from the car. At that, the phone went in the kitchen, and I went off to answer it. While I was on the phone, he fetched his box and, unbeknownst to me, began playing it. Suddenly, I had one ear on the phone call and one on this sound that was coming from the bar. One of the waitresses walked in and I asked her what the music was. She told me that it was the guy I had been speaking to, playing his accordion.

'Never,' I said. I couldn't believe it. I finished my phone call, walked through and sat down, with my eyes popping out of my head. I could hardly believe what I was hearing. I had never heard such genius, musicality, fingering, call it what you like, in my life.

He stopped playing and I said, 'My goodness, I'm the last person that you want to be playing a tune with.'

'Oh no,' he said, 'I really want to go home and say that I've played a tune with Fergie MacDonald.'

He persuaded me to get my accordion out.

'Easy on,' said I, 'you'll have to come down to my level.'

We proceeded with 'John MacMillan of Barra' and a few other standards like that. He loved it and we kept on playing. Then he looked out and saw the clay-pigeon layout in front of the hotel.

'Oh, I would love a go at the clay pigeons,' he exclaimed.

So I took him out, and he blootered away at the clays for a while. I have to say that he was pretty good at that too. We eventually came back inside, and he said, 'We cannot possibly allow you to be banished to the wilderness.'

'How do you mean?' I said.

'You must start playing your box again. It's a must. I'll tell you,' he said, 'I'm helping to put together a programme on the television, and I'm going to recommend that you come on board.'

I used to know the music business inside out. You meet so many people who tell you how they are going to 'help you' and how they are going to 'promote you'. Invariably, you never hear another cheep from them again. I thought that this was one of these guys, but, lo and behold, he was on the phone within a week. He told me that the programme was indeed going ahead on the BBC, and that it was to be called *Tàlla a' Bhaille* (The Village Hall). He said that it was being directed by John Smith, from the island of Lewis, and that the two of them had decided that I should get a young band together, to play my own brand of traditional ceilidh music.

That is exactly what happened. I gathered a crowd of youngsters round me, ably supported by a couple of 'old heads' in the shape of Davy Flockhart on piano, and Alistair MacLeod on double bass. The rest of the band included guys like Iain MacFarlane, Allan Henderson, Colm O'Rua, Iain MacDonald (Glenuig) and Allan MacColl. Most of these lads were youngsters who hadn't broken into anything at that stage. They were, of course, over the moon to be coming along with me.

That was really the start of things again. We did the show, and suddenly letters and phone calls began to pour into the BBC wanting more. So I got that group together again, and we got back in on the recording scene. We played this brand of music which I liked so much; real good, old-fashioned stuff, but played by these brilliant young musicians with a very modern outlook and an understanding of how the whole traditional music scene was progressing. We left behind us the shackles of Scottish country dance music and were completely uninhibited, bringing in instruments that were so much frowned upon by the purists. We had the usual boxes, fiddles and drums, but we backed that up with whistles, banjos, flutes and small pipes.

It was shortly after this that BBC Radio Scotland became aware of this born-again version of Fergie MacDonald, who was hitting the headlines. As you know, they had stopped me from broadcasting that very same type of music many years before. Here they were, however, inviting me back onto such programmes as the Scottish dance music broadcast, 'Take the Floor', to play my very own brand of ceilidh music. As one might say, the wheel had turned full circle, although they still do not generally accept this kind of thing. Mine is probably the only real ceilidh band broadcasting at the moment. My music, although tolerated, is still looked on by many as a deviation away from the regular strict tempo music which is still the mainstay of Scottish dance broadcasts. I go out of my way to put together a programme that is relaxing, easy on the ears, nothing complicated, but steeped in the West Highland Gaelic traditions.

This sudden surge of popularity got me back playing at ceilidhs, dances and balls all over the Highlands and Islands once more. It was great to be back on the road. In addition to this, I started doing regular television and radio work again, and I'm very honoured (thankful to the Lord in fact) that a man of my age isn't crippled with arthritis, or any of these ailments which would restrict me from playing music.

In many ways, my comeback (if I can call it that) has become one big trip down memory lane. For example, I was playing recently at a dance in Bonar Bridge hall. It suddenly dawned on me that this hall had an amazing story attached to it, involving Fergie. I had forgotten all about this incident, as I had not played in that hall for almost forty years. It brought back a lot of good memories.

The year was 1965, a Saturday night dance in Bonar Bridge. I was a young band leader, and I took an awful fancy to a beautiful dark-haired young girl, who I had spotted dancing round the floor. At the end of the night we met somehow. She actually came up for an autograph as I recall. I decided to be direct, and I asked her if I could see her home from the dance. I was so delighted when the young lady agreed. I was over the moon, and I asked the other boys to pack away the gear while I saw the young lady home. That wasn't a problem, so I escorted her to the car and away we went. We had just left the hall, when I asked her in which direction I was to go; where did she live? To my horror, the answer was Scourie, sixty miles away. Well, I nearly ejected through the roof.

I hadn't the heart to say, 'Oh dear me, I've made an awful mistake, you'd better go home with the rest of your friends.' I just couldn't do it. It took hours to drive over there and back. Needless to say, when I returned I wasn't exactly flavour of the month with the rest of the band, who were still waiting for me at the hall. Boy, did I not catch it? They were fuming! Strangely enough, this initial marathon led to a romance, and I am happy to say that the young lady and I are still firm friends to this day.

When I came back into music I realised that the whole scene had changed dramatically from the one which I had left. For a start, there were fewer dance bands playing north of Crianlarich. There a vacuum had been created. Really, the dancing scene and dance music were pretty much on the back burner.

I looked at the situation very very carefully, and sussed out that ceilidh music was the road I should choose. I believed that my own Gaelic music, mixed with a smattering of Irish, would prove an irresistible cocktail. I went headlong into the process of building around me a group of young, up and coming, hotshot musicians, who were of a like mind musically. In addition to those mentioned above, I was also able to call on the services of Iain MacColl on guitar, Iain Joseph MacDonald on accordion and Hugh MacCallum and David MacKay on drums. I was lucky enough to have a very large pool in the Moidart and Lochaber area, and fortunately, being youngsters, they were very keen and were dying to learn their trade.

I moved away from the mainstream line-up of two accordions, fiddle, piano and drums, and went instead for a real ceilidh band sound, which included button box, fiddle, banjo, flute, whistle, keyboard and drums. I realised that getting all these instruments in the mix would provide the basis for a good-going dance outfit. You will never achieve the sound of a ceilidh band if you stick to the instruments used in your average Scottish country dance band. The change of sound is vital. The choice of music is of equal importance.

A lot of the youngsters that started off with Fergie have now advanced on to greater things. They themselves have become big names in the world of traditional music, and this gives me a great lift. I am so happy and delighted to see them all at the forefront of things. Having said that, I obviously still have my 'road band', which I love, but when the chips are down, and anything big happens, they are still the first boys I call. They have been brought up with Fergie almost, and have known my music since they could walk. Really, we never rehearse. There is no need to. We just fit into each other musically, without any problem whatsoever.

I have been joined in the band recently by members of my own family. This really pleases me. Angela is left running the hotel, while her sister, Morven Ann, who has developed into a very competent piano player, travels the country with me. My son, John, is following in his father's footsteps with his button box. In my opinion, John is a really good musician, but what makes me really happy, is that his style is his own. He does his own thing, plays his own music and very rarely touches on mine, though I do hear some of my own techniques being employed sometimes. It looks as if John and Morven have quite a future in the music world.

In fact, John is the man behind one of my best known trademarks in recent years. He was a very talented football player, and a big Manchester United fan. When he was playing locally he used to wear his 'United' strip, complete with red stockings. One particular night, I was going away somewhere to play, and I could not find a pair of socks to wear. Eventually I just grabbed the first ones I found, which turned out to be John's red football socks. I threw them on and away I went.

The dance was in Inverness, and an awful lot of people came up and commented on the red socks, though I never told them why I had them. It seemed to tickle the fancy of a lot of folk. Very shortly after that I went to the Pan Celtic Festival in Tralee, in Ireland, and while I was over, I bought another pair of red socks for no particular reason at all. I started wearing them at lunchtime sessions while I was playing in the local 'Brogue Bar'.

The BBC Scotland Gaelic department was represented at the festival by Morag MacDonald, from the island of South Uist, who presents her own programme, called *Mire re Mòr*, on *Radio nan Gàidheal* every morning. She was really taken up with the socks, and it developed into a bit of a running joke; 'Fergie and the Red Socks'. Now it has reached the stage that wherever I am playing, women lift up my trouser leg to see if I am wearing red socks. Morag MacDonald is constantly plugging this on her radio broadcasts. When she is introducing a track from one of my albums she refers to me as *Fear nan Stocanan Dearg*, 'Man of the Red Socks'. If you live in the Highlands, you will know that that is Fergie, which suggests that she has a lot to answer for, although it has added a brand new dimension to me, and I am associated everywhere with red socks. There are some occasions when I forget to put them on, and this causes consternation in village halls all over the Highlands. People come up and ask me where they are, and it is amazing the phone calls that Morag MacDonald gets, to tell her that Fergie was not wearing his red socks. It has really become a big part of my life.

There are, as you now know, a number of different parts to my life and, at the moment, I am working on a number of projects. There is a video being made about me, I am working on a CD release and the BBC are currently making a documentary film about my music. There is also the small matter of this book that you are reading.

Up until recently, I had never dreamt of writing a book of memoirs, because I had really never stopped long enough to have a good look at myself. I just always carried on with life, without ever giving any consideration to the things I had done or experienced. But over the last few years so many people, from all walks of life (members of Parliament to members of my own family) have been on at me to do just that, although I don't suppose I ever really paid any attention to them.

I suppose it began to start working on my mind at some point, and after that I did give it some careful consideration. Eventually, I began to take stock of myself, and with the help of a few friends, who reminded me of so many stories and anecdotes, I decided that it would be a good idea to jot down a few of my memories and observations.

Since the inception of this book, it has dawned on me that I have lived a very full life. Not a moment has been wasted. Life hasn't passed me by; most definitely not, and that leaves me in a very fortunate position. There have been so many different facets to my life that I have been forced to gloss over much of what I have crammed into my 65 years.

Perhaps someone will carry out a more detailed investigation of my past in years to come.

This is only the tip of the iceberg, and has been, to all intents and purposes, only a glance back. I have spent very little time looking at more recent passages of my life. It would be fair to say that since I have started playing again, there have been so many more incidents and accidents, tales and stories. Who knows? Maybe this will be the subject of future volumes. That, as they say, is for another day!

Roll of Honour

What follows is a list of musicians who have played with Fergie MacDonald during his career. The list is roughly chronological but by no means exhaustive. We apologise now for any names omitted.

***Fiddle Players** from 1950 to 1960*

Archie MacNaughton	Acharacle
John MacDonald (Seonaidh Ailean)	Dorlin
Farquhar MacRae	Roshven
Jimmy Manuel	Salen
Dr Frank Davidson	Salen
Dougie MacRae	Ach an Eilean
Donald MacRae	Ach an Eilean
Roddy MacDonald	Langal

From 1960 to 1970

Jimmy Yeaman	Dundee
Derek Auld	Perth
Gavin MacIntyre	Glasgow
Farquhar MacRae	Roshven
Aonghas Grant	Lochailort
Willie MacGregor	Perthshire
Hamish MacGregor	Lochearnhead

From 1970 to 1980

Aonghas Grant	Fort William
Iain Henderson	Glen Affric
Iain Kennedy	Lochyside
Alec Ross	Lochailort
Charlie MacFarlane	Glenfinnan

From 1980 onwards

Farquhar MacRae	Roshven
Iain MacFarlane	Glenfinnan
Allan Henderson	Mallaig

***Drummers** from 1950 to 1960*

'Wee Archie'	Glasgow
Iain MacNaughton	Newton of Ardtoe
Alistair MacAuley	Dalilea

From 1960 to 1970

Mike Dowds	Glasgow
Eric Simmons QC	Glasgow
Billy Grant	Glasgow
Jay Dewar	Strathyre

From 1970 to 1980

Billy Thom	Dunblane
John Hunter	Wick
George Bremmner	Portree
Keith Eadie	Mallaig
Tosh Campbell	Fort William
Dochie Stewart	Acharacle
Sandy Stitt	Fort William
George Young	Mallaig
Gilbert Stevenson	Islay

From 1980 onwards

David MacKay	Strontian
Allan MacColl	Corpach
Hugh MacCallum	Inverlochy
Angus MacColl	Benderloch
Duncan Gillespie	Islay

Fraser MacInnes	Tobermory

***Box Players** from 1950 to 1960*

Dr Frank Davidson	Salen
Lachie John MacEachan	Dorlin
Donald MacColl	Dorlin
Farquhar MacRae	Roshven
Geordie Watt	Kirriemuir

From 1960 to 1970

Farquhar MacRae	Roshven
Gordon Fraser	Glenborrodale
Alasdair Clark	Fort William
Alastair Henderson	Portree
Lex Keith	Glasgow
Calum Ross	Taynuilt
John Carmichael	Glasgow
Archie MacKillop	Harris
Iain MacLachlan	Benbecula
George Smith	Mull

From 1970 to 1980

David Bowen	Inverness
Willie Lawrie	Ballachulish
Hecky Henderson	Fort William
Farquhar MacRae	Roshven
Iain MacLachlan	Benbecula
Iain Ewart	Glasgow
Willie Cameron	Acharacle

From 1980 onwards

Farquhar MacRae	Roshven

Addie Harper Jnr.	Wick
John Carmichael	Glasgow
Jim Johnstone	Edinburgh
Jock Fraser	Inverness
Allan MacColl	Corpach
Alastair MacCuish	Glasgow
Michael Garvin	Oban
Charlie MacLeod	Glasgow
John F. MacDonald	Mingarry
Iain Joseph MacDonald	Roy Bridge
Angus MacPhail	Tiree
Iain MacLachlan	Benbecula
Jimmy Joe MacDonald	Knoydart
Sandy Meldrum	Stornoway
Phil Cunningham	Hollywood

Piano and Keyboard Players *from 1960 to 1970*

Fiona MacLaren	Glenborrodale
Ian Lawrence	Glasgow
Calum Kenmuir	Helensburgh
Graham Hannah	Glasgow
Alma Kerr	Stornoway
Willie Lawrie	Ballachulish

From 1970 to 1980

Belle Henderson	Fort William
Hecky Henderson	Fort William

From 1980 onwards

Violet Morrison	Stornoway
David Flockhart	Tobermory
Isabel Harper	Wick

Jock Fraser	Inverness
Mary Adam	Glenborrodale
Morven Ann MacDonald	Mingarry
Iain Joseph MacDonald	Roy Bridge
Allan Henderson	Mallaig
Ingrid Henderson	Glenfinnan
Gordon Middler	Aberdeen
Dave Berry	Fife
Mark MacDougal	Muir of Ord
Bill Hendry	Perth
Sandy Meldrum	Stornoway

***Guitar Players** from 1960 to 1970*

Donnie MacArthur	Stornoway
Bob ?	Shetland
Johnny Hamilton	Glasgow
Noel Eadie	Glasgow
Alastair Forbes	Glasgow

From 1970 to 1980

Johnny MacLean	Fort William
Mike McGruer	Fort William
Graham Leck	Mallaig
James Manson	Mallaig
Tony MacCuish	Fort William
Sandy MacIntosh	Fort William

From 1980 onwards

Duncan Findlay	Glasgow
Iain MacColl	Corpach
Addie Harper Jnr.	Wick
Clen MacKenzie	Wick

***Banjo Players** from 1960 to 1970*

Malky McCormick	Kilmarnock

From 1970 to 1980

Allan Savage	Newcastle

From 1980 onwards

Duncan Findlay	Glasgow
David (Dagger) Gordon	Easter Ross
Joseph Cunningham	County Galway
Colm O'Rua	Dublin
Addie Harper Jnr.	Wick

***Bass Players** from 1960 to 1970*

Johnny Cochran	Glasgow
Bob Eadie	Glasgow
Noel Eadie	Glasgow
Alastair Forbes	Glasgow

From 1970 to 1980

Hecky Henderson	Fort William
James Manson	Mallaig

From 1980 onwards

Alastair MacLeod	Tobermory

***Vocalists** from 1960 to 1970*

Johnny Hamilton	Glasgow
Noel Eadie	Glasgow
Maureen Duffy	Motherwell
Cameron MacKichan	Glasgow

From 1970 to 1980

Tony MacCuish	Fort William
Mike McGruer	Fort William
Robert MacMillan	Mallaig

***Whistle and Flute Players** from 1980 onwards*

Iain MacDonald	Glenuig
Iain MacFarlane	Glenfinnan
Allan Henderson	Mallaig
Duncan Nicholson	Fort William

***Highland/Small Pipes and Chanter Players** from 1980 onwards*

Iain MacDonald	Glenuig
Allan MacColl	Corpach
Duncan Nicholson	Fort William
Allan MacDonald	Glenuig
Allan Henderson	Mallaig
David MacGillivray	Mingarry
David MacKay	Strontian
Jonathan Stewart	'The Gorge', Glencoe
Kenneth MacDonald	Glasgow

***Jews Harp** from 1960 to 1970*

Angus Lawrie	Oban